Sustainable Urban Transport Financing
from the Sidewalk to the Subway

A WORLD BANK STUDY

Sustainable Urban Transport Financing from the Sidewalk to the Subway

Capital, Operations, and Maintenance Financing

Arturo Ardila-Gomez and Adriana Ortegon-Sanchez

WORLD BANK GROUP

Contents

Figures

Tables

Acknowledgments

The authors would like to thank the World Bank for providing the initial funds to write this book. Also, we thank peer reviewers Shomik Raj Mehndiratta and Victor M. Vergara for their careful review and comments, as well as anonymous reviewers at the World Conference on Transport Research and the Latin American Congress on Urban Public Transport (CLATPU), who provided comments on earlier drafts. Leonardo Canon, Harvey Scorcia, and Anita Shrestha provided support, comments, and suggestions as the research effort evolved. Invaluable editorial assistance was provided by Anna van der Heijden. Aurelio Menendez, Indu John-Abraham, Maria Dolores Arribas-Banos, Thierry Desclos, Om Prakash Agarwal, Nancy Vandycke, Sara Sultan, Alejandro Hoyos, Kirti Devi, and Luciana Silva also supported this effort. Financial support for the finalization of this book was provided by PPIAF, which is a multidonor trust fund that provides technical assistance to governments in developing countries to develop enabling environments and to facilitate private investment in infrastructure. For more information on PPIAF visit: http://ppiaf.org.

About the Authors

Arturo Ardila-Gomez is Lead Transport Economist in the World Bank Group's Transport and ICT Global Practice. He comanages the Urban Mobility Global Solutions Group at the Bank. He oversees a portfolio of transport projects and research activities in China, Ecuador, and Mongolia and provides overall technical support to the East Asia transport portfolio, in particular Vietnam. He also supports projects and peer reviews extensively for all regions in the Bank. Prior to joining the Bank, he was director of the Transportation Studies Group at Los Andes University in Bogota, Colombia. He is the author of several peer-reviewed articles and a book. He is currently finishing research on Smart Cities, ITS, Mobility, and Energy Efficiency.

Adriana Ortegon-Sanchez is a researcher at the Centre for Transport Studies and the Accessibility Research Group in University College London-UCL. She conducts research on visions for future sustainable and liveable cities and studies the interaction between urban environments, mobility, and well-being. She is involved in sustainable transport policies' analysis and capacity-building projects in Colombia, Cuba, Panama, and Peru, providing advice and training for low-carbon mobility policies and nonmotorized transport strategies in cities. Before joining UCL she worked as a consultant for the World Bank and the Inter-American Development Bank on transport financial sustainability and gender mainstreaming in public transport systems. She has extensive experience working on conceptual designs of integrated transport systems in Colombian cities.

Executive Summary

Urban transport systems are essential for economic development and improving citizens' quality of life by providing access to places and activities for work, education, services, or leisure. To establish affordable as well as high-quality transport systems, cities must ensure their transport systems are financially sustainable: revenue must be enough to pay for new investments in infrastructure while also funding maintenance and operation of existing facilities and services.

Cities' underfunding trap. Currently, many cities in developing countries are stuck in an "underfunding trap" for urban transport. In these cities, the up-front investments that are needed for new transport infrastructure are huge, while revenue from their still small-scale and perhaps even poor-quality systems and other sources is insufficient to cover maintenance and operation expenses, let alone new investment projects. The urban transport financing gap in these cities is further widened by the implicit subsidies for the use of private cars, which represent only a minority of trips but contribute huge costs in terms of congestion, sprawl, accidents, and pollution. Current literature presents several strategies for cities to address this urban transport financing gap, but individual strategies only partially address its complex causes.

Proposed analytical framework to assess and design urban transport financing. In this book, an analytical framework is proposed to support the design of comprehensive urban transport financing. Based on the concept of "Who Benefits Pays," the framework presents a standardized approach for analyzing and assessing available financing mechanisms (such as public sector funding, farebox revenue, road tolls, or land value capture mechanisms) based on beneficiaries (general public or direct and indirect beneficiaries), funding periodicity, and financial and transport sustainability. Within the framework, financial sustainability is determined in terms of stability, political acceptance, and administrative ease of instrument implementation, while transport sustainability is measured in terms of economic efficiency, social equity, and environmental impact. The book also uses the concept of making *wise* investments, which are investments that can decrease the funding gap by adding benefits and reducing expenditures, especially over time.

Analysis of potential financing instruments. Using the framework, 24 types of potential financing instruments are assessed in terms of their ability to fund urban transport capital investments, operational expenses, and maintenance. The analysis highlights the instruments' individual strengths and weaknesses, but also points to general trends for categories of instruments based on beneficiary type.

The findings suggest that instruments that charge the *direct* beneficiaries of urban transport investments, such as passengers or drivers, may be politically and administratively inconvenient but efficiently achieve sustainable transport goals. In financial terms, these direct benefit instruments generate a continuous revenue flow that can be used to address capital, operation, and maintenance requirements. Charging *indirect* beneficiaries, such as developers and landowners, is found to be slightly less efficient in terms of transport sustainability, but a generally stable and convenient way to raise a large sum up front for capital investments. Finally, the analysis of *general* benefit instruments underscores that sustainable transport projects bring major economic, social, and environmental benefits and thus could be funded by national or international institutions on behalf of society. In this context of *general* benefits, however, only public transport (not private-vehicle infrastructure) projects generate sufficient benefits to justify society paying for their capital, operation, and maintenance costs. Private-vehicle infrastructure needs to be financed through instruments that charge the direct beneficiaries.

For cities that are investing in transport, the framework analysis also underscores the need to base urban transport financing on an appropriate mix of complementary financing instruments, possibly involving multiple levels of government and different sectors. In particular for capital investments, a combination of grants and loans from funding agencies combined with investments through public–private partnerships could finance large projects that benefit society. Moreover, the property tax emerges as a key financing instrument for capital, operation, and maintenance expenses.

Achieving comprehensive and sustainable urban transport financing. By choosing the most appropriate sets of financing instruments and focusing on wise investments, cities can design comprehensive financing for all types of urban transport projects, using multilevel innovative revenue sources that promote efficient pricing schemes, increase overall revenue, strengthen sustainable transport, and cover capital investments, operation, and maintenance for all parts of a public transport system, "from the sidewalk to the subway."

Abbreviations

BRT	Bus Rapid Transit
CDM	Clean Development Mechanism
CER	Carbon Emission Reduction
CODATU	Cooperation for Urban Mobility in the Developing World
CTF	Clean Technology Fund
DIF	Development Impact Fees
GDP	gross domestic product
GEF	Global Environment Facility
GIZ	German International Cooperation
ITS	intelligent transport systems
JD	Joint Development
NE	Negotiated Exactions
PPP	Public–Private Partnership
PROTRAM	Transportation Federal Support Program (Mexico)
TDM	Transport Demand Management
TIF	Tax Increment Financing
TUF	Transportation Utility Fee

Introduction

In many cities in developing countries, urban transport is characterized by severe congestion and low-quality public transport. While a majority of trips is made by public transport, trips take a long time. Meanwhile, with only a minority of trips made by private vehicles, streets are congested and roads in poor condition. This congestion and poor road quality are affecting economic development and further hurt public transport—typically used by the poor and less affluent—as buses also need to use the congested lanes. In addition, the urban development pattern is further hurting the poor as they live farther away from job centers, and their neighborhoods are frequently developed informally with precarious road networks, sidewalks, and other urban infrastructure. The low quality of these public transport systems, the relatively small scale of the transit networks, and the poor condition of roads and sidewalks indicate that these urban transport systems do not have the financial resources to cover all costs, including capital investments and operation and maintenance expenses. This large and increasing financing gap for urban transport is currently seen as the main difficulty faced by cities trying to improve their transport systems.

Indeed—as described in more detail in chapter 1—many cities in developing countries are stuck in an "underfunding trap" for urban transport. In these cities, the up-front investments that are needed for new transport infrastructure are huge, while revenue from their still small-scale and perhaps even poor-quality systems and other sources is insufficient to cover maintenance and operation expenses, let alone new investment projects. The urban transport financing gap in these cities is further widened by the implicit subsidies for the use of private cars, which represent only a minority of trips but contribute huge costs in terms of congestion, sprawl, accidents, and pollution. While cars generate more costs than benefits and public transport actually generates more benefits than costs, explicit subsidies for public transport are subject to political controversy, while the implicit subsidies for cars are not. Current literature presents several strategies for cities to address this urban transport financing gap, but individual strategies only partially address its complex causes.

In this book, an analytical framework is proposed and applied to support comprehensive financing for urban transport systems, especially for cities in developing countries that need to close a growing financing gap. Based on the concept of "Who Benefits Pays," the framework presents a standardized approach for analyzing and assessing available financing mechanisms based on beneficiaries (general public or direct and indirect beneficiaries), funding periodicity, and financial *and* transport sustainability. The book also uses the concept of making *wise* investments, which are investments that can decrease the funding gap by adding benefits and reducing expenditures, especially over time.

This book is organized in two parts.

Part 1: Comprehensive and Sustainable Urban Transport Financing. Part 1 begins with a description of the main challenges to urban transport financing and the key factors that are causing cities to experience an underfunding trap (chapter 1). Chapter 2 then presents the analytical framework, based on the "Who Benefits Pays" principle, which can be used to assess urban transport financing instruments and design comprehensive financing. Key results for different groups of instruments—direct benefit, indirect benefit, and general benefit instruments—are presented in chapter 3. Next, chapter 4 builds on the framework results of chapter 3 (as well as on the individual assessments in part 2), to discuss how the various instruments could and in fact should be combined to finance different modes and elements of the transport system, providing key recommendations for designing comprehensive urban transport finance schemes based on the framework findings. Finally, chapter 5 summarizes the results of the framework implementation in an overall conclusion.

Part 2: Financing Instruments. The second part of this book presents the more detailed and systematic analysis of 24 financing instruments using the standard analysis framework introduced in part 1. While the findings in part 1 are based on an "average" or the "most common" characteristics of each financing instrument, the results of the framework analyses in part 2 present a more nuanced description for each. In this part, the analyses of the instruments are organized by the instruments' type of beneficiary—general, indirect, and direct benefit instruments—with additional information provided for each of those categories of instruments. Chapter 6 on general benefit instruments covers public transport subsidies, property taxes, national and international loans and grants, as well as climate-related financing instruments. Direct and indirect benefit instruments are covered in chapters 7 and 8, respectively. Direct benefit instruments, for example, include parking charges and road pricing, while indirect benefit instruments cover advertising and employer contributions, as well as various value capture instruments. Lastly, chapter 9 discusses public–private partnerships (PPP).

PART 1

Sustainable Urban Transport Financing

CHAPTER 1

Challenges for Urban Transport Financing and Cities' "Underfunding Trap"

Model Analysis of Urban Transport Finance Investments for Cities of Different Scale

To illustrate the size and scope of the financing challenge for urban transport systems, a stylized model of an urban transport system, covering public transport as well as private cars, can be used. To start with, the infrastructure needs for various modes of transport increase dramatically with city size. Depending on their size, cities need to invest in various amounts (expressed in kilometers or kilometer-lane) of bus transport, Bus Rapid Transit (BRT), metro lines, local roads, sidewalks, and—in the case of larger cities—express ways (table 1.1).

Next, expenses not only grow with city size but also depend on a city's stage of network evolution (figure 1.1). In cities still developing their urban transport systems (left side of figure 1.1), large capital investments are typically still needed to expand the network, while maintenance and operation costs are somewhat lower. As networks grow, capital investments generally go down, while costs for operation and maintenance increase with the size of the network.

Table 1.1 City Sizes and Associated Transport Infrastructure

in km or km-lane

	Area	BRT	Metro	Local roads	Express roads
City	(blocks)	(km)	(km)	(km–lane)	(km–lane)
Medium	50 X 50	25		2,000	40
Large	250 X 250	150	50	50,000	600
Mega	500 X 500	400	250	200,000	1,500

Source: Authors based on model analysis.
Note: BRT = Bus Rapid Transit.

Figure 1.1 Typical Pattern of Capital, Operation, and Maintenance Expenditures for Transport

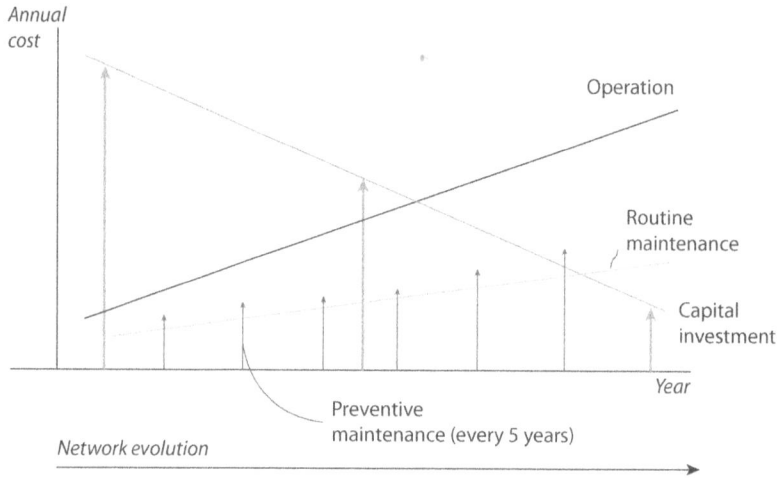

Source: Authors based on model analysis.

Figure 1.2 Total Estimated Costs (Capital, Operation, and Maintenance) for Medium, Large, and Mega Cities over 20 Years

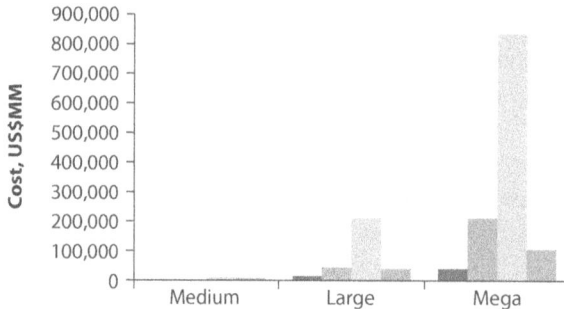

	Medium	Large	Mega
■ BRT	2,505	15,030	40,080
▨ Metro	0	41,750	208,750
▨ Local roads	8,350	208,750	835,000
▨ Express roads	2,672	40,080	100,200

Source: Authors based on model analysis.
Note: BRT = Bus Rapid Transit.

Maintenance in figure 1.1 is included as both routine (every year) and preventive (every five years) maintenance.

The combined effects of table 1.1 and figure 1.1 are illustrated in figure 1.2, capturing the total estimated costs for capital investments, operation, and maintenance over a 20-year period for medium, large, and mega cities, based on the model analysis. Figure 1.2 underscores the huge expenses involved, in particular

Figure 1.3   Infrastructure Needs (a) and Estimated Total Cost of Capital and Maintenance (b) for Bogota's Road Network over 20 Years

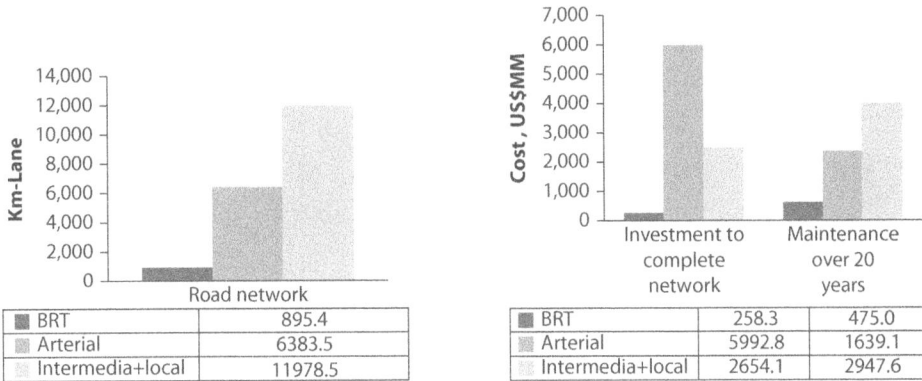

	Road network
BRT	895.4
Arterial	6383.5
Intermedia+local	11978.5

	Investment to complete network	Maintenance over 20 years
BRT	258.3	475.0
Arterial	5992.8	1639.1
Intermedia+local	2654.1	2947.6

Source: Ardila-Gomez and Ortegon-Sanchez 2013.
Note: BRT = Bus Rapid Transit.

for the network of local streets that provide the ultimate access to all places within a city. As cities grow, these costs for local roads increase exponentially as each additional city block demands roads on all four sides.

The huge expenses for local road networks are also illustrated by the application of the model to real data from the road network in Bogota, Colombia (figure 1.3). With the city at an early stage of network evolution, the figure illustrates Bogota's need to still make large capital investments to extend its road and mass transport networks. Having to make these capital investments while also maintaining a large and growing road network, however, presents a huge financial responsibility for the city.

The comparison of the stylized model with data from a real city also shows that a city's financing needs are larger, given the informal pattern of urban development that most cities in developing countries have followed. In this pattern, a significant share of urban growth takes place through slums that lack proper roads, sidewalks, and other urban infrastructure. These slums need to be retrofitted with higher costs than if space for those facilities had been spared when the areas were developed. Land acquisition for roads and other transport facilities, moreover, becomes a significant expense. These cities therefore tend to have a "spatial viability gap," which complicates not only transport but also the introduction of all urban services. To minimize the long-term cost of urbanization, transport is clearly a sector that needs to be addressed early on in the urban transformation sequence as the costs of not planning for transport early are enormous.

Insufficiency of Revenue Sources and the Underfunding Trap

As illustrated in the example of Bogota, for cities still at an early stage of their network development, the large expenses for capital investments combined with already large and growing costs for maintenance and operation can create an

Figure 1.4 Schematic Representation of a City's Underfunding Trap based on Empirical Data for the Bogota Transport System

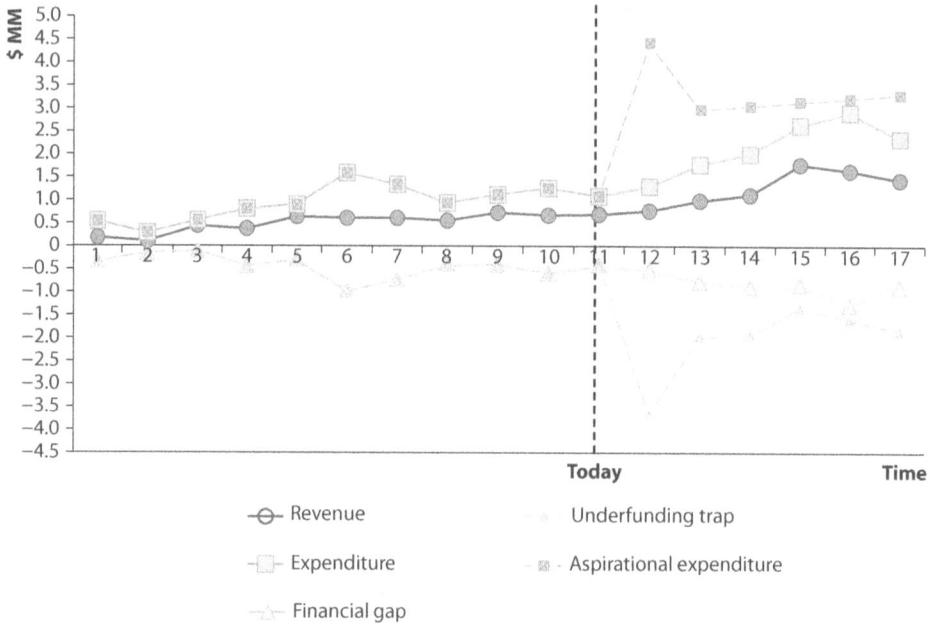

Source: Ardila-Gomez and Ortegon-Sanchez 2013.

Note: Expenditure does not include operational costs as operation of the Bogota transport system has been mostly financially self-sustainable.

"underfunding trap" in terms of transport financing (figure 1.4). While expenses are high, revenue generation is typically limited as a result of the poor quality and small size of the transport network.

Using data from the Bogota transport system, figure 1.4 illustrates both the city's financing gap (the difference between revenue and expenditures) and its "underfunding trap." The underfunding trap in the figure is the difference between revenue and the city's ideal or "aspirational expenditure" for its road network, which represents the ideal investment level for completing planned capital investments and performing routine and preventive maintenance to keep the network in good condition. Without the resources to complete investments and properly maintain and run the system, Bogota and other cities are trapped in a situation of large expenses and insufficient revenue.

In table 1.2, several possible sources of funding for urban transport systems are listed, showing more traditional sources, such as general taxes that flow to the budget, along with emerging ones. In principle, because public transport is a public service and transport infrastructure is a public asset, governments have been expected to be able to afford transport investments through their public budgets, relying primarily on taxes and user fees.[1] In reality, however, with generally insufficient transport system revenues, cities have already turned to other sources to try to cover the financial gap.

Table 1.2　Main Revenue Sources in Urban Transport

Type	Sources
From the public sector: Managed by main agents in areas such as infrastructure and operation.	General budget funded through general taxation.
	Loans from banks or funding agencies.
	Grants from international funding agencies or bilateral aid.
From users: Paid by users of the different modes who pay for the service they are receiving.	Ticket fees by public transport users.
	Payments by users of individual motorized vehicles, such as tolls for the use of infrastructure (bridges or urban motorways), congestion charges to access areas such as city centers, parking charges, taxes on fuels, and fines (if the country's legislation has earmarked the source).
	Vehicle ownership tax (allocated to transport when permitted by legislation).
	Payments by users of soft modes of transport, such as bicycles, for example, rental charges when using self-service systems or secure lock-ups.
From other people: Various contributions by people who benefit from the improvements and effects generated by a transport system, even if they are not users.	Payroll tax for private companies whose employees make use of the system (in some countries, such as France, this is 0.5–2.6 percent of payroll).
	Contributions in the form of direct assistance to the employee when a firm covers a share of employees' daily transport costs (such as the *Vale transporte* in Brazil).
	Taxes on land value increases for local residents and traders (such as betterment levies in Colombia).
	Recovery of a share of capital gains to fund mobility.

Source: Authors based on CODATU 2009.

Four key factors contribute to the revenue shortage, as mentioned in the literature:

- Limitations of existing financing mechanisms to generate sufficient revenue. Existing financing for urban transport is mostly based on traditional revenue sources such as investments from the general tax base, public transport user fees, and farebox revenue. Considering the huge and sunk costs of capital investments and the high expenses for operation and maintenance, these traditional sources are insufficient. Although other sources are available (see table 1.2), they are not yet widely used and still do not generate enough revenue.
- Inefficient pricing and economic distortions (Medda 2011; Zegras 2006; Zhao, Das, and Larson 2012). While public transport is in great need of investments, implicit subsidies are provided to the road network and private cars. Cars represent only a minority of users and trips, yet expansions of the road network are carried out with funding from the general tax base. Moreover, car users are not paying for all costs associated with driving in terms of the congestion and

pollution caused by private vehicles. Cars also benefit from fuel subsidies and other implicit subsidies, such as when street parking is provided free of charge (Gomez-Ibanez 1999; Haubold 2014; TransitCenter and Frontier Group 2014).

- Unbalance in investment responsibilities and financial capacity at the city level. Decentralization has generally strengthened local administration, but while municipalities have been empowered in terms of their expenditure *responsibilities*, there has been little movement by national governments to implement a strategy that would give the municipalities more budgetary self-sufficiency (Bahl, Linn, and Wetzel 2013).[2] As a result, city governments may lack the financial autonomy to pay for the services they are required to provide, for example if they lack capacity to expand local revenues through property or sales taxes.

- Mismatch between the periodicity of revenue and expenditure. The nature of transport systems requires both large and up-front capital investments, as well as recurrent and relatively smaller expenses for operation and maintenance. While cities grow incrementally, investment needs vary greatly over time, as the needed expenses for transport infrastructure development are not gradual but lumpy. Operations and maintenance expenditures are needed, moreover, if this infrastructure is to yield the expected benefits during its lifetime. The search for alternative funding sources, however, has generally focused more on the need for capital investments. A sound financial system would have revenue sources that can address both kinds of expenditures.

The inefficient pricing and economic distortions in the transport sector are further illustrated in figure 1.5, which depicts the explicit and implicit costs of cars compared to public transport. When the implicit costs of externalities are included, the costs of cars are greater than their benefits. Not only in the daily operation of the transport network but, more significantly, in the long term,

Figure 1.5 Total Costs (Explicit and Implicit) and Benefits of Cars and Public Transport

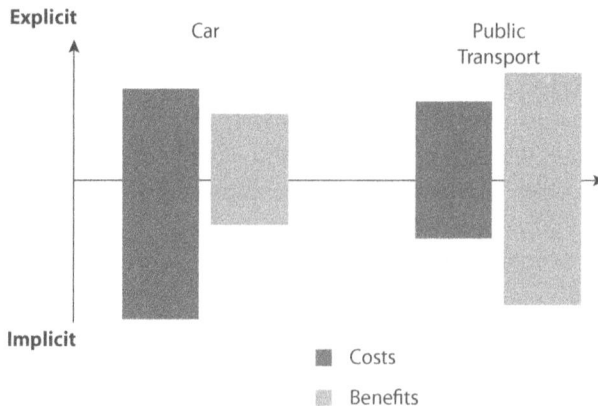

Source: Authors.

through the impacts on urban development created by the ongoing investments in road infrastructure designed for cars. Such investments, which are implicit subsidies to cars, typically facilitate sprawl and urban realm designs not favorable for people, which ultimately makes it more complex and expensive to provide good public transport networks.

Public transport also receives subsidies,[3] but these tend to be more explicit as they appear more conspicuously in most city budgets. As such, they are more readily subject to political controversy. In addition, public transport tends to have higher benefits than costs because of its capacity to efficiently carry large volumes of passengers. However, despite public transport's better cost-benefit ratio and the likely effect of the implicit subsidies for private cars to further increase the deficit of the transport system, politically the balance is still against public transport and in favor of private transport.

Finally, in addition to the four causes of the underfunding trap discussed in current literature, the development of sound and comprehensive financing schemes is further complicated by two characteristics of urban transport system financing: (i) conflicting economic rationales for those who must provide transport services, given their public and private good characteristics;[4] and (ii) the diversity of funding sources, including private and public sectors and different levels of government (local, national, global). While existing financing mechanisms for transport infrastructure rely heavily on public finances—based on the idea that transport is a public service that should be publicly provided—transport has both public and private good characteristics, a fact that could favor the argument that public transport infrastructure should not be exclusively publicly financed. The second complication relates to the unbalance between political decentralization and financial decentralization and the wide range of available funding sources from different sectors (public and private) and government levels. This makes the selection of appropriate funding more difficult, unless the advantages and disadvantages of each level are clearly understood.

Moving forward, the design of urban transport system finances should take into account these various factors that contribute to the underfunding trap or otherwise complicate urban transport system finances. Until recently, the main—if not the only—objective and criteria for selecting financing instruments and funding sources was to increase the transport sector's income. Although increasing revenue remains a main objective of financing schemes, sustainable and comprehensive financing requires a different understanding of financing sources.

Impacts of Transport Underfinancing on Economic Development and Urban Poor

The current underfunding of city transport systems comes at a cost beyond that of just having poor-quality transportation. As addressed above, the recurrent implicit subsidies for cars are adding future transportation development costs as a result of urban sprawl. In addition, major costs are associated with poor maintenance and congestion. Public transport users—usually the poor and the bottom 40 percent by income—disproportionately suffer from being stuck in traffic; congestion is therefore regressive as it unreasonably affects the users of public transport. Poorly maintained roads also slow down buses and cars, damage vehicles, and cause accidents. In addition, the usual pattern of development in poor areas of cities in developing countries means that these areas—the slums—lack proper roads and sidewalks. As a result, the poor find it difficult to access jobs because of the lack of infrastructure in their neighborhoods and because of being stuck in traffic in poor-quality transport. On top of this, poor people are more likely to be injured in accidents (Nantulya and Reich 2002) and a household can fall into poverty for three generations if the main breadwinner is lost to an accident (The Economist 2014). Lastly, not investing enough in an urban transport system can also decelerate a city's rate of economic growth. An analysis of Chinese metropolitan regions found a statistically meaningful relationship ($R^2=0.68$) between meters of expressway per square kilometer and gross domestic product (GDP) per square kilometer, using a sample of 49 metropolitan regions in China (Leman 2014).[5]

Partial Strategies in Current Literature

Current literature presents various strategies to address the transport system financing gap. Strategies are mainly focused on three key areas: (i) analyzing and combining different types of (existing) financing instruments, (ii) exploring new financing instruments, and (iii) addressing pricing distortions.

In the first line of research, researchers have taken a wide approach to analyze all types of financing mechanisms. Sakamoto,[6] for example, argues that the part of the urban transport system that promotes environmental sustainability can raise enough revenue to cover all its costs. His approach focuses on the analysis of financing mechanisms, classified by government levels, to define a financing strategy that achieves sustainability through a combination of multilevel financing instruments that reflect the real costs of transport, integrates financing into a wider policy, and overcomes political and economic barriers.

Along the same lines, the comprehensive approach by Cooperation for Urban Mobility in the Developing World (CODATU) also uses an analysis of the main financing instruments to define a financing strategy that combines instruments and has all costs borne by a certain party. CODATU in particular focuses on the institutional capacity required to support an innovative financing strategy, arguing for the involvement of levels of government above the city level—for example, the national government—to help cover much-needed capital costs. The CODATU approach, however, does not explicitly cover the recurrent costs for operations and maintenance.

In a second line of research for addressing the urban transport financing gap, it is argued that the potential extra revenue capacity of existing financing instruments is limited, which means that new mechanisms, such as, for example, a tax surcharge earmarked for the urban transport system, need to be created (Gwilliam 2000; Gwilliam 2002). This approach, however, tends to be politically acceptable only for megaprojects, such as metros, and typically for capital costs. Moreover, when accepted for elements of the transport system, the sole existence of earmarked sources can hinder—paradoxically—the use of other sources of revenue that could also finance the transport system on the grounds that a large and steady source of funding is already available—even if it is insufficient. As part of this line of research, many authors (Calimente 2012; Junge and Levinson 2012; Lari et al. 2009; Medda 2011; Peterson 2009; Zegras 2006) have focused on analyzing specific types of financing mechanisms such as land value capture instruments or public–private partnerships (PPPs), analyzing them as effective pricing strategies to raise revenue and redistribute the investment responsibilities and risks among different sectors for specific projects.

Finally, the literature highlights the need to correct urban transport pricing distortions and increase revenue by making users pay the full cost of services and incentivize efficient demand levels for the different modes. However, a practical framework to build a path toward this objective has not yet been thoroughly developed. Although the literature that focuses on specific financing mechanisms develops conceptual frameworks to analyze efficient pricing and revenue increases, analyses do not consider the impact of the mechanism on overall financial or transport system sustainability.

While all three lines of research provide valuable findings and insights, from the perspective of providing comprehensive urban transport financing, however, the current literature only seems to address separate parts of a larger, more complex problem. Building on the existing literature, the framework presented in the next section aims to address the larger issue of urban transport underfinancing by incorporating multiple sources of revenue and analyzing its various characteristics in terms of beneficiaries, periodicity, financial sustainability, transport sustainability, and suitability for financing.

Notes

1. This book distinguishes between taxes and user charges or fees. The revenue collected from taxes goes to a general fund that pays for all government services, regardless of their name. Taxes are therefore not earmarked to cover certain government services. For example, taxes such as vehicle tax are levied on cars, but the revenue does not go to the transport system directly. User fees, on the other hand, charge for the use of a facility or for a specific service and therefore the revenue collected goes to cover costs associated with that service of facility (Bahl and Linn 1992); (Farvacque-Vitkovic and Mihaly 2014); and (Bahl, Linn, and Wetzel 2013).

2. Most subnational government expenditures in developing countries are financed through transfers, although in a few cases (such as the Philippines, Brazil, and Colombia) a third or more of the subnational government expenditures are financed from own source revenues. (In these cases, regional and/or local governments usually have access to some form of taxation on business transactions, in addition to a

property tax (Bird and Slack 2004). The transitional countries are a special case. They have always passed a significant level of responsibilities to the subnational governments, but usually devolved very little revenue raising power. China is perhaps the extreme example, with subnational governments having almost 70 percent of expenditure responsibility but essentially no independent taxing power (Bahl and Bird 2008). As described by (Meloche, Vaillancourt, and Yilmaz 2004), "decentralization of expenditures coming with centrally controlled revenues seems to be an obstruction to economic growth."

3. See also chapter 3 and table 6.1.

4. A public good is defined as a good for which the benefits are nonexclusive. This means that a person cannot appropriate himself or herself of all the benefits the good offers, nor can he or she prevent others from using it; a classic example of this is the sun or national defense. A second attribute of public goods is their nonrivalry, which means that additional units of the good can be consumed at zero social marginal cost of production. Examples of nonrivalry include an extra viewer tuning into a television channel or an extra car using an empty road. However, roads lose their nonrivalry attribute when congested. On the contrary, private goods are rival and excludable (Nicholson and Snyder 2008).

5. See also Kamal-Chaoui, Leman, and Zhang (2009).

6. See Sakamoto and Belka (2010).

CHAPTER 2

Analytical Framework for Urban Transport Financing from the Sidewalk to the Subway

Framework Overview

To improve urban transport financing, an analytical framework is proposed for the design of *comprehensive* urban transport financing. The framework is based on the concept of "Who Benefits Pays" and builds on existing literature, case studies, and practical experiences with urban transport financing, particularly in Latin America, to address several aspects of a city's underfunding trap and other complexities of urban transport financing schemes. Specifically, the framework addresses the following elements that are explained below in more detail:

- Economic distortions, through application of the "Who Benefit Pays" principle
- The need for *wiser* investments, which can reduce the financing gap in the long term
- Financial *and* transport sustainability
- Periodicity of revenue and expenditures, specifically for capital, operation, and maintenance expenses.
- Public and private sector investments and involvement of different levels of government.

After an introduction to the main concepts of the framework, the results of a framework analysis of 24 common and emerging financing instruments is presented in chapter 3. The framework aims to provide a standardized approach to analyze instruments and thus enable cities to determine the best set of complementary instruments for achieving sustainable urban transport *and* financial sustainability.

Who Benefits Pays

A key aspect of the proposed analytical framework is its use of the "Who Benefits Pays" principle, which states that those who benefit from a transport service or urban transport improvement should pay for its costs. Although highly dependent on the context of each city, generally, transport projects will create three types of benefits: (i) general benefits, which are received by society in general and—according to the principle—therefore must be paid by public authorities as representatives of the general public; (ii) direct benefits, which are received mainly by users of the transport system and can be directly charged to them; and (iii) indirect benefits, which are received by people that are nonusers of the system but still perceive benefits from the improvements in accessibility, mobility, and increases in business opportunities associated with the development of transport projects.

Different instruments can be used to target these beneficiaries and seek payment for the services or added value from the transport improvement. An overview of financing instruments by type of beneficiary is presented in table 2.1.

When planning for an urban transport investment, the project's benefits should be identified and measured so that they can be paired with specific financial instruments to capture the added value that is created and ensure the main beneficiaries pay for it. This way, urban transport financing can be based on an efficient revenue scheme in which charges, fees, and taxes reflect prices that cover the costs of using any specific infrastructure (Zegras 2006) or service, ensuring all costs are borne by a certain party (CODATU 2009). Moreover, the share of cost financed (for transport infrastructure or transport services) should be proportional to the benefit received (Lari et al. 2009).[1] Because the principle

Table 2.1 Financing Instruments by Type of Beneficiary

General benefit instruments	Direct benefit instruments	Indirect benefit instruments
Beneficiary: General public	*Beneficiary: Direct Beneficiaries (users, drivers, passengers)*	*Beneficiary: Indirect beneficiaries (firms, land and property owners, developers)*
Public transport subsidies	Parking charges	Advertising
Property taxes	Road pricing	Employer contributions
National and international grants and loans	Congestion charges	Added value capture mechanisms
	Fuel taxes and surcharges	Land-value taxes/betterment levies
Climate-related financial instruments	Vehicle taxation	Tax increment financing
Global Environment Facility (GEF)	Farebox revenue	Special assessment
Clean Technology Fund	PPPs for urban roads	Transportation utility fees
Clean Development Mechanism (CDM)		Land asset management
Public–Private Partnerships (PPPs) for public transport		Developer exactions
		Development impact fees
		Negotiated exactions
		Joint developments
		Air rights

Source: Authors.

requires the identification of the type of benefit, it also provides guidance for when the payments should be made, such as in the form of an initial lump sum or recurrent payment.

Wise Investments: Sustainable Financing and Sustainable Transport

In addition to the focus on "Who Benefits?," a second key aspect of the proposed framework is the concept of *wise* investments and its related focus on financing instrument attributes in terms of both sustainable *financing* and sustainable *transport*. Wise investments are defined as investments that in the long run reduce a city's financing gap by supporting projects that are cost effective, increase benefits and revenue and limit costs, and may also attract other financial benefits.

At the moment, without a focus on wise investments, governments that want to develop their transport system basically choose between building more roads and investing in mass transit (Zegras 2006), with the final decision mostly depending on funding availability. However, when the full costs of such investments would be considered—particularly in terms of impacts on urban form,[2] sprawl, spatial and social segregation, the exclusion of low-income populations, and overall economic growth (CODATU, 2009)—investment choices may well change. This is because the provision of infrastructure and services to low-density, car-dependent cities requires larger capital investment in the short term along with increased long-term needs for the maintenance and operation of the expanded road network and mitigation of externalities such as pollution and congestion. Alternatively, sustainable, inclusive, low-carbon modes, such as mass transit or nonmotorized modes, promote a more compact urban form that facilitates efficient use of scarce resources such as land, promoting articulated densification processes that can have positive impacts on economic vitality, access to opportunities, and overall prosperity of the city.

Moreover, investing in sustainable transport projects and good-quality transportation can start a virtuous cycle in which cities become more attractive for investments by different actors (such as the national government or international agencies) or even other sectors, further supporting the transport system's overall financial sustainability. A good example of a transport project attracting national government investments is the Transmilenio BRT project in Bogota, Colombia (Ardila-Gomez and Ortegon-Sanchez 2013).

While any capital investment will require long-term financing for preventive and routine maintenance and to cover operational costs, wise investments can increase the cost-effectiveness of projects in terms of their social and economic benefits and in terms of finances, by attracting more financing. The concept of wise investments further also relates to a consideration of how financing instruments themselves influence transport supply and demand, for example by changing travel behavior and by encouraging service suppliers to find technological alternatives. In general, the concept of wise investments highlights the broader impact and context of investments. It requires governments to untie financing requirements from specific projects and their corresponding budgets and move toward identifying long-term planning objectives, appropriate economic instruments, and necessary changes in policies and institutions to achieve their stated goals.

Complementary Sources of Revenue and Addressing Periodicity

The complexity and huge costs involved with urban transport financing also require investments to rely on multiple, complimentary sources of revenue. Different instruments will have different strengths and weaknesses, which may be balanced out by combining sets of revenue sources for larger transport investments. For example, for services with private good characteristics, governments should charge user fees when beneficiaries can easily be identified. Conversely, where user fees are difficult to estimate, taxes and transfers would be more appropriate. Governments can thus design a blend of funding sources according to the variety of services provided (Bird 2001), which can come from different government levels based on the local political and institutional context.

Blending financing instruments is also important to address the periodicity of needed expenditures. While capital investments are huge and up front and can take advantage of economies of scale, other expenses, such as operation and maintenance costs, are relatively small and periodic or ongoing and depend on the number of users, population size, inflation, or other factors. As discussed in chapter 1 (figure 1.1), the amount of resources and type of financing instruments required are largely related with the level of development of the transport network (Sakamoto and Belka 2010). Highly developed transport networks would have mainly recurrent operational and maintenance expenditures, while less developed transport networks will still be requiring large capital investments in the short term and recurrent funding sources in the long term. For financial sustainability, financing instruments must respond to the time variations of expenditures.

Notes

1. A common standard to define user fees, known as the "rational nexus test," includes the following criteria: (i) the service must be directly attributable to those bearing the cost; (ii) the costs must be allocated proportionally to the benefits; (iii) the facilities funded must be part of a comprehensive plan; (iv) the fee must account for taxes paid toward transportation, so property owners are not double billed; and (v) the fee revenues must be used for their intended purpose in a timely manner (Altshuler et al. 1993), as cited by (Junge and Levinson 2012).

2. As described in (Kopp, A., R. Block, and A. Iimi 2012), "the durability of transport equipment, the longevity of its infrastructure, and high fixed costs mean that current investments lock in the modal structure of transport for decades."

CHAPTER 3

Framework Analysis of Public and Private Financing Instruments

Overview

Using the key framework characteristics described in chapter 2, an analysis was made of the 24 financing instruments (table 2.1) that could be used to finance urban transport projects. Table 3.1 illustrates the exact attributes that were addressed for each instrument, including the type of benefit and beneficiaries, as well as strengths and weaknesses related to financial and transport sustainability and appropriateness to fund capital, maintenance, or operational expenses. Each financing instrument was analyzed using information from literature, case studies, and project and personal experience.[1]

The overarching results presented in this and the next chapter are based on an "average" assessment of each instrument, while more detailed and nuanced information for each are presented in part 2. The exact applicability of each instrument will always depend on the context and situation of a particular city and transport investment, but the assessment of instruments—the overall

Table 3.1 Summarized Analysis Framework for Evaluating Urban Transport Financing

General characteristics	
Benefit	Type of benefit (general, direct, or indirect) and amount of the benefit that can be "captured" by the instrument.
Beneficiary/funder	Agent receiving the benefit; according to the "Who Benefits Pays" principle, the agent perceiving the benefit must therefore also fund the mechanism.
Level of government involved	Level of government (local, national, or international) in charge of managing the instrument.
Type of expense	Capital, maintenance, or operation
Periodicity	Temporal behavior of the revenue generated by the instrument (up-front (a one-time revenue), recurrent, or both).

table continues next page

Table 3.1 Summarized Analysis Framework for Evaluating Urban Transport Financing *(continued)*

Financial sustainability

Stability	The level of stability indicates whether or not an instrument is robust. If stability is high, the instrument's application will only require moderate variations over the long term, with the instrument relatively unaffected by economic cycles (be it cyclical or countercyclical), thus supporting long-term planning. Stability is also associated with buoyancy and how an increase in the use of the transport resource affects its revenue (Simon and Nobes 2009).[a]
Political and public acceptability	Political acceptability relates to how clearly or not the instrument's benefits and characteristics (such as adoption, implementation, and tax burden) can be identified and accepted by the general public. The size of the base rate (as an indicator of the amount of people that might have to pay the tax) can also be a measure of acceptability.
Convenience and administrative ease	Convenience and administrative ease relate to the efficiency with which the instrument can be implemented, considering instrument administration and compliance, which typically use a portion of the instrument's revenue. Convenience also depends on the number of agents involved in the instrument's management and associated transaction costs.

Transport sustainability

Efficiency	Specifically related with economic efficiency, this attribute evaluates the effectiveness of the mechanism in terms of correcting the effects of existing economic distortions caused by market failures. Corrective "charges" internalize the externalities generated by transport projects by assessing the externalities caused by individuals and charging a cost equivalent to the benefits those individuals are receiving. Efficiency also evaluates the instrument's ability to equate marginal benefits to marginal costs of development.
Equity	Associated with fairness, this attribute refers to horizontal and vertical equity. Horizontal equity means that individuals who are in "essentially similar economic circumstances" are treated the same and pay the same. Vertical equity, with regard to income and social class (Litman 2014), defines that individuals who have a greater ability to pay or receive greater benefits should pay more (Bird and Slack 2004). Equity is therefore related to the effect of the financing mechanisms on different populations groups, such as different income groups or groups in different locations or even different generations. Related to different income groups, the distributive effect can be either progressive (if the instrument favors disadvantaged groups) or regressive (if otherwise) (James and Nobes 2009).
Environmental impact	Environmental impact is related with the environmental effects of the financing mechanisms and their capacity to correct distortions and amend the adverse effects of transport on the environment (Button 2010). The attribute evaluates if the instrument helps internalize external costs and promotes investment in sustainable transport modes and strategies.

Other considerations

Associated risks	Although any risk or effect from a certain charge depends on the local context, common important risks can be identified and highlighted for policy makers based on experiences with the instruments in different locations. Risks include unexpected secondary effects that can have negative consequences for the instrument's financial or transport sustainability.

Source: Sakamoto and Belka 2010; Zhao and Levinson 2012; Litman 2012. Definitions for the attributes are based on (Sakamoto and Belka 2010) and (Mikesell 2003), as cited by (Junge and Levinson 2012) and (Lari et al. 2009).

a. Buoyancy of a financing instrument is defined as the ratio between the increase in revenue collected and the increase in GDP. Revenue levels will reflect the effects of any changes, including discretionary changes to the instrument's structure.

findings in part 1 and the detailed assessments in part 2—point to the general strengths and weaknesses of instruments, which can help cities define optimum combinations of complementary financing instruments that fit their particular situation and objectives.

Measure of Benefits and Funding Periodicity

Tables 3.2, 3.3, and 3.4 present an overview of analysis findings in terms of the key benefits, government levels, and funding periodicity typically associated with each of the financing instruments reviewed. Organized by type of beneficiary—general public, direct beneficiaries, or indirect beneficiaries (see chapter 2)—the tables specify the measure of benefit and whether the instrument is suitable for up-front or recurring costs, or both. In general, financing instruments with recurrent revenues can finance operation and maintenance expenditures, while financing instruments that generate large lump sums up front can be used to cover capital investments for new infrastructure.

The findings in table 3.2 underscore that sustainable transport projects bring major economic, social, and environmental benefits to the general public's overall

Table 3.2 Financing of Capital, Operations, and Maintenance using General Benefit Instruments

Beneficiary	Financing instrument	Gov level	Cost	Measure of benefit	Up front	Recurrent
Society	**Public Transport Subsidies**	L/N	M/O	Accessibility, equity, environmental health		●
				Increases in productivity, economic growth		
				General tax base growth		
	Property Tax	L/N	C/M/O	Increases in productivity, economic growth		●
				General tax base growth		
	National and International Loans and Grants	L/N/G	C/M	Increases in productivity, economic growth	●	●
				General tax base growth		
	Carbon Market	G	C/O	Greenhouse emission reductions	●	●
	Global Environment Facility	G	C/O	Greenhouse emission reductions	●	
	Clean Technology Fund	L, N	C	Greenhouse emission reductions		●
	PPPs for Public Transport	P/L/N	C/M/O	Accessibility, equity, environmental health.	●	●
				Increases in productivity, economic growth		
				General tax base growth		

Source: Zhao and Levinson 2012.
Note: L = local government; N = national government; G = global institutions; P = private sector; C = capital investment; M = maintenance; O = operations; PPPs = public–private partnerships.

well-being and consequently can be funded by national or international institutions on behalf of society. In this context, however, only public transport projects (not those for private-vehicle infrastructure) generate sufficient benefits to justify society paying for them.

Table 3.3, which summarizes results for direct beneficiaries such as transit users and drivers, shows that financial instruments funded by direct beneficiaries are recurrent, given that they are directly related with the use of the system. As a result, it then seems both politically and administratively correct that these instruments are mainly managed from a local level and used for recurrent expenditures such as operation and maintenance.

Unlike the direct benefit instruments, financing instruments funded by indirect beneficiaries (table 3.4) do not show a direct relationship between periodicity and level of government involved. Since most are related with the

Table 3.3 Financing of Capital, Operations, and Maintenance using Direct Benefit Instruments

Beneficiary	Financing instrument	Gov level	Cost	Measure of benefit	Up front	Recurrent
Users/Drivers	**Parking Charges**	L	C/M/O	Zonal access rights		●
	Road Pricing	L	C/M/O	General access rights		●
	Congestion Charges	L	C/M/O	Demand controlled access rights		●
	Fuel Taxes/ Surcharges	N	C/M/O	Gas consumption/ driven miles		●
	Vehicle Taxation	L/N	C/M/O	Owned vehicles/types		●
Users/Passengers	**Farebox Revenue**	L/P	O/M	Ridership, amount of trips, accessibility		●
Users	**PPPs for Urban Roads**	P/L/N	C/M/O	General access rights	●	●

Source: Zhao and Levinson 2012.
Note: L = local government; N = national government; G = global institutions; P = private sector; C = capital investment; M = maintenance; O = operations; PPPs = public–private partnerships.

Table 3.4 Financing of Capital, Operations, and Maintenance using Indirect Benefit Instruments

Beneficiary	Financing instrument	Gov level	Cost	Measure of benefit	Up front	Recurrent
Firms	**Advertising**	L/P	M/O	Sales increases due to more exposure		●
Firms	**Employer Contribution**	L	M/O	Use of public transport by employees		●
Land/property owners	**Betterment Levies**	L/N	C/M	Land value growth/property tax growth	●	●
Land/property owners	**Tax Increment Financing**	L	M/O	Property tax revenue growth (within TIF district)	●	

table continues next page

Table 3.4 Financing of Capital, Operations, and Maintenance using Indirect Benefit Instruments *(continued)*

Beneficiary	Financing instrument	Gov level	Cost	Measure of benefit	Up front	Recurrent
Land/property owners	**Special Assessment**	L	M/O	Assessed special benefits	●	
Developers	**Transportation Utility Fees**	L	M	Transportation utility		●
Developers	**Development Impact Fee**	L/N	C	Off-site development opportunities	●	
Developers	**Negotiated Exactions**	L	C/M/O	On-site access benefits	●	●
Developers	**Joint Development (PPP)**	L/N	C	Development privileges	●	●
Developers	**Air Rights**	L/N	M/O	On-site development opportunities	●	●

Source: Zhao and Levinson 2012.
Note: L = local government; N = national government; G = global institutions; P = private sector; C = capital investment; M = maintenance; O = operations; TIF = tax increment financing; PPP = public–private partnership.

development of real estate projects, it is expected that large up-front sums are generated at the initial stages of the projects, and ongoing revenue will be obtained once the projects start operations.[2]

Revenue Levels and Financial and Transport Sustainability

The application of the framework to the 24 financing mechanisms also generated insights into their individual strengths and weaknesses in terms of financial and transport sustainability, as well as general trends in those areas for the different categories of instruments. In the framework, financial sustainability is addressed by analyzing the instrument's stability, public acceptance, and administrative ease, while transport sustainability is expressed in terms of efficiency, equity, and environmental impact (see also table 3.1). Revenue level is presented mostly in an indicative manner to give a relative order of magnitude of revenue levels for the different financing instruments.

Tables 3.5, 3.7, and 3.8 summarize the findings for the 24 instruments, adding potential revenue levels and information on the level of achievement (high: green; medium: yellow; and low: red) for each attribute of financial or transport sustainability. The findings are again organized by type of beneficiary—general public, direct, and indirect beneficiaries, with examples of practical applications provided for many of the instruments.

General Benefit Instruments
For general benefit instruments (table 3.5), results show that national and international loans and grants perform well across all attributes for financial and transport sustainability. Also notable are the similarities in attribute strength for

Table 3.5 Revenue Levels and Financial and Transport Sustainability of General Benefit Financing Instruments

Financing instrument	Rev level	Financial sustainability			Transport sustainability			Cost	Period	Beneficiary
		Stability	Public accept	Admin ease	Efficiency	Equity	Environ. impact			
Public Transport Subsidies	▁▃▅	♣	•	♦	♦	•	♦	M/O	◊	Society
Property Tax	▁▃▅	•	♦	♦	♣	♦	♣	C/M/O	◊	Society
National and International Loans and Grants	▁▃▅	•	•	♦	•	•	•	C/M	♠	Society
Carbon Market	▁▃▅	♣	•	♣	♦	♦	•	C/O	♠	Society
Global Environment Facility	▁▃▅	♣	•	♦	♦	♦	•	C/O	*	Society
Clean Technology Fund	▁▃▅	♦	•	♦	♦	♦	•	C	◊	Society
PPPs for Public Transport	▁▃▅	♦	•	♣	♦	•	•	C/M/O	♠	Society

Source: CODATU 2009; Sakamoto and Belka 2010; Zhao, Das, and Larson 2012.
Notes: Symbols indicate the level of achievement by an instrument for each attribute: • = high; ♦ = medium; and ♣ = low. L = local government; N = national government; G = global institutions; P = private sector; C = capital investment; M = maintenance; O = operations; PPPs = public–private partnerships.

the environment- and climate change–related instruments. The property tax is worth mentioning because of its broad use and stability.

The financing instrument "national and international loans and grants" performs very well overall, as the agencies providing this funding are concerned with sustainability attributes and typically also support institutional and technical capacity development along with the delivery of funds. National grants and loans are widely used in the United Kingdom, the United States, and Mexico, among other countries. The United Kingdom has eight types of funds for different types of projects, with funds awarded via competitive bidding. In particular outside London, where public transport is provided in deregularized markets, these funds can be used to support operators with operational costs or to subsidize social routes that are not commercially viable. In the United States, the federal government provides grants for capital investments for busways or trams that will be planned, implemented, and operated at the local level.[3] In Mexico, the federal government's Transportation Federal Support Program (PROTRAM) gives study grants and loans for the complete funding of capital costs of public transport projects. Table 3.6 summarizes the main characteristics of several national programs that primarily finance public transport.

While clearly scoring "high" in terms of environmental impact, both the carbon market and Global Environment Facility (GEF) instruments have a medium impact on equity issues and generally low performance regarding financial stability.[4] Ratings on equity relate to the fact that for both instruments funding generally goes to projects that promote cleaner public transport systems and nonmotorized transport modes, which in developing countries is used mostly by the lower-income population; the instrument thus has some impact on equity. Financial stability is low because these funds have rarely financed urban transport projects (Kopp, A., R. Block, and A. Iimi 2012).

Table 3.6 Main Elements of National Support Programs for Urban Transport Projects

	United States	Germany	France	Colombia	Mexico
Jurisdiction responsible for urban transport	Municipalities (alone or in combination), Metropolitan Planning Organization (MPO)	States (Länder) and municipalities	Municipalities (local transport authorities (AOUTs)> 100,000 habitants).	Municipalities, creating management bodies	States and municipalities to which the state has given the responsibility
Regulatory framework of federal support	Federal laws. Federal partnership with municipalities	Municipal Financing Act of Transportation	Interior Transportation Act, the Air Act, Urban Renewal Act	National law and central government-city agreements	Decree creating the National Infrastructure Fund; and agreement that creates the PROTRAM
Origin of resources (primary source)	Surcharge on fuel, budgetary contributions	Fuel surcharge	Transport rate, aimed at local authorities	Future budgetary funds	Trust highways and federal resources
Agency administrator	Federal Transit Administration and Department of Transportation, with regional offices	Ministry of Transportation	Ministry of Transport (local offices) and other	Ministry of Transport, National Planning Department	Ministry of Communications and Transport and Banobras
Criteria, tools, programs	70% by formula (% investment), 30% discretionary, for Capex 10 programs	80% by formula, 20% projects	General criteria for eligibility	BRT and integrated transit systems for cities 600K+ integrated transit system in smaller towns	General criteria for eligibility
Annual contributions (funding and budget)	US$9 billion	US$1.50 billion (same amount for urban roads)	Approximately US$6 billion (2 billion for Île de France)	ND	ND
Receptors main resources	Regional transport authorities	Länders, who transfer to municipalities	Local transport authorities (AOUT)	Cities	States, cities
Requirements for eligibility of projects	Short-term strategic urban plans, detailed project planning	Urban transport plan, secured cofinancing	Urban integration, project planning, alternative	System manager, conceptual plan, consistent with PND and POT	PIMUS and project is 35% private funding

table continues next page

Table 3.6 Main Elements of National Support Programs for Urban Transport Projects (continued)

	United States	Germany	France	Colombia	Mexico
Evaluation criteria	Scores of 1–5, merits of the project and cofinancing	Cost-benefit analysis	Economic and social assess- ment	Cost-benefit analysis and other criteria	Cost-benefit analysis and other criteria
Maximum-limit federal funding per project	80%	75%	35% (20% under- ground lines)	70%	50%

Source: Ardila-Gomez 2012.
Note: PIMUS: Plan Integral de Movilidad Urbana Sustentable or Sustainable Urban Mobility Integral Plan (Mexico); PROTRAM: Programa Federal de Apoyo al Transporte Masivo or Transportation Federal Support Program (Mexico); PND Plan Nacional de Desarrollo or National Development Plan (Colombia); POT: Plan de Ordenamiento Territorial or Urban Master Development Plan (Colombia).

As illustrated in table 3.5, subsidies to public transport perform reasonably well across all attributes (except stability). Subsidies for public transport can be for capital investments or operations and maintenance. In general, subsidies are needed to at least cover capital costs because of the large lump sums required to build a metro or a bus rapid transit line. In contrast, for operations and mainte- nance—as well as some capital costs such as those for fleet– efficient pricing should lead to covering costs. The review in this book, however, found that sub- sidies for operation and maintenance are frequently used, often as a subsidy to the provider of the service ("supply-side subsidies"). Supply-side subsidies can have negative incentives and could be used to mostly cover operators' inefficien- cies. If subsidies must be used, fares should be set to cover as much of the costs as possible, and subsidies should go to the users, as "demand-based subsidies." Demand-based subsidies allow targeting the neediest in society while having those with enough income pay for the service. Therefore, subsidies for public transport are recommended to be used either for capital costs or—if used for operating costs—for the "demand side" only. Therefore, the use of subsidies needs careful consideration as it could go against the "Who Benefits Pays" principle. To avoid public subsidies contributing to economic distortions, subsidies should be coupled with regulations to guarantee that they are not used to compensate private sector inefficiencies. As (Estupinan et al. 2007) and (Gwilliam 2002) sug- gest, public transport operating subsidies support equity and efficiency only in very particular and limited circumstances. The rationale for qualifying subsidies as an appropriate financing tool then only works if society as a whole is getting the benefits from the accessibility provided by the transport system, which is only true if the transport system provides good quality, high coverage, and inclu- sive accessibility. Thus, the objective of the subsidies for public transport cannot be just to provide lower fares, especially not at the expense of quality and quan- tity of transport supply.[5] Instead, subsidies must guarantee inclusion and afford- ability to specific segments of the population (such as low income, children, and elderly). In addition, and equally important, subsidies can be used to achieve high-quality integrated transport systems if the level of subsidy is defined within a contract-regulated service to remunerate operators for pursuing noncommercial, strategic, and social objectives according to quality performance indicators,[6] as in the case of London or Santiago de Chile.[7]

Direct Benefit Instruments

The main findings of the direct benefit instruments are presented in table 3.7. As might be expected, the instruments are well suited to support sustainable transport goals as they, of all instruments, most directly represent the "Who Benefits Pays" principle. Most of the instruments are also good revenue sources, providing a steady flow of revenue appropriate for operation and maintenance. While farebox revenue only shows a mostly medium performance for all attributes, it is an important instrument as it is almost exclusively designated to cover the operational and maintenance costs of the system. Table 3.7 also illustrates that almost all direct benefit instruments score low in terms of political acceptability. This finding might relate to the difficulties of charging a fee for something that is considered a "right" and therefore erroneously perceived as "free" in terms of out-of-pocket expenses.

Because of the recurrent nature of the revenue from these instruments, the instruments will perform best when locally managed and conceived within a comprehensive transport strategy. Global examples of successful

Table 3.7 Revenue Levels and Financial and Transport Sustainability of Direct Benefit Financing Instruments

Financing instrument	Rev level	Financial sustainability			Transport sustainability			Cost	Period	Beneficiary
		Stability	Public accept	Admin ease	Efficiency	Equity	Environ. impact			
Parking Charges	ⅷ	♦	♣	♦	●	●	♦	C/M/O	◊	Users/Drivers
Road Pricing	ⅷ	♦	♣	♦	●	●	●	C/M/O	◊	Users/Drivers
Congestion Charges	ⅷ	♦	♣	♣	●	●	●	C/M/O	◊	Users/Drivers
Fuel taxes/ Surcharges	ⅷ	●	♣	●	●	●	●	C/M/O	◊	Users/Drivers
Vehicle Taxation	ⅷ	♦	♣	♦	♦	●	●	C/M/O	◊	Users/Drivers
Farebox Revenue	ⅷ	♦	♦	♣	♦	♦	♦	O/M	◊	Users/Passengers
PPPs for Urban Roads	ⅷ	♦	♦	♣	♦	♦	♦	C/M/O	♠	Users

Source: CODATU 2009; Sakamoto and Belka 2010; Zhao, Das, and Larson 2012.
Notes: Symbols indicate the level of achievement by an instrument for each attribute: ● = high; ♦ = medium; and ♣ = low. L = local government; N = national government; G = global institutions; P = private sector; C = capital investment; M = maintenance; O = operations; PPPs = public–private partnerships.

local management of instrument revenue include congestion charges in Singapore and London; a congestion/pollution charge in Milan; fuel taxes in the United States, Colombia, and Germany; and parking charges:

- Singapore's congestion charge is managed by the Land Transport Authority, which transfers the revenue to the central government.
- London's congestion charge is managed by Transport for London, the integrated transport authority, and funding is reinvested in the public transport system. London's congestion charge gross revenue in 2007/08 was approximately US$400 million, of which 48.6 percent was used to cover operating costs and the remainder invested in improving the bus network, infrastructure, and safety (Sakamoto and Belka 2010).
- In Milan, the *Zona C* congestion/pollution charge collected nearly US$28 million in 2012, of which 36 percent were used to cover operating costs, 49 percent invested in improving metro and services and surface transport (buses and trams), and 15 percent on the expansion of the cycle hire scheme *BikeMi* (54 new docking stations and 3,300 new bicycles).[8]
- Fuel taxes in the United States are managed at the level of individual states. In California, around 70 percent of the tax revenue goes to transport; of this 10 percent goes to public transport and road maintenance (CODATU 2009).
- In Bogota, Colombia, fuel taxes are earmarked, 50 percent of total fuel taxes revenue goes to capital investments of BRT lines, 40 percent to capital and maintenance of the road network, and 10 percent to local councils for maintenance of local roads (Ardila-Gomez and Ortegon-Sanchez 2013).
- In Germany, fuel taxes are managed at the federal level; in the state of Bavaria, they are used to subsidize 40 percent of operating costs of suburban rails (CODATU 2009).
- For parking charges, the share of total revenue varies widely among cities. In San Francisco, parking charges are managed by the San Francisco Municipal Agency and represent a third of its total revenue (CODATU 2009). In Tanzania, parking is managed by a private firm and represents almost 25 percent of total revenue (Wright 2007). In Barcelona, parking charges are managed by the city's transport authority and used as the main source of funding for the city's *Bicing* bicycle sharing scheme. In London, parking charges and fines on local roads are managed by the councils; parking fines have been decriminalized so that the councils can directly collect this revenue and invest it in public transport and environmental projects (CODATU 2009).

Indirect Benefit Instruments

The summarized finding of the framework analysis of the indirect benefit instruments are presented in table 3.8. Most of the financial mechanisms in this category other than the advertising and employer contributions are land- or property-related value capture mechanisms, which follow similar rationales but have important differences in design and implementation. Analysis results

Table 3.8 Revenue Levels and Financial and Transport Sustainability of Indirect Benefit Financing Instruments

Financing instrument	Rev level	Stability	Public accept	Admin ease	Efficiency	Equity	Environ. impact	Cost	Period	Beneficiary
Advertising	▂▃▄	●	●	♦	♣	♣	♦	M/O	◊	Firms
Employer Contribution	▂▃▄	●	♦	♦	♦	♦	♦	M/O	◊	Firms
Betterment Levies	▃▄▅	♦	♣	♣	♦	♦	♦	C/M	*	Land/Property owners
Tax Increment Financing	▃▄▅	●	●	♣	♦	♣	♦	M/O	*	Land/Property owners
Special Assessment	▂▃▄	♦	♦	♣	♦	♣	♣	M/O	*	Land/Property owners
Transportation Utility Fees	▂▃▄	♦	♣	♣	●	♣	♦	M	◊	Developers
Development Impact Fee	▃▄▅	♦	♦	♦	♦	♦	♣	C	*	Developers
Negotiated Exactions	▃▄▅	♦	♦	♦	♦	♦	♣	C/M/O	♠	Developers
Joint Development (PPP)	▃▄▅	♦	♦	♣	●	♦	♦	C	♠	Developers
Air Rights	▃▄▅	♦	♦	♣	♦	♣	♦	M/O	♠	Developers

Source: CODATU 2009; Sakamoto and Belka 2010; Zhao, Das, and Larson 2012.
Notes: Symbols indicate the level of achievement by an instrument for each attribute: ● = high; ♦ = medium; and ♣ = low. L = local government; N = national government; G = global institutions; P = private sector; C = capital investment; M = maintenance; O = operations; PPP = public–private partnership.

suggest that with appropriate design and management, land-based value capture financing is a good alternative to widen the tax base and ensure continuous revenue for local or central governments. The instruments generally are good for generating large amounts of money up front, and thus for capital investments. As shown in table 3.8, some of the instruments show good levels of revenue, but medium performances on both financial and transport sustainabilities, with the lowest performance observed for equity and administrative ease.

The instruments' overall medium performance on stability is related to the fact that developer exactions mechanisms, such as development impact fees, negotiated exactions, joint development, and air rights, all depend on the real estate market, which in turn is highly dependent on economic conditions. Betterment levies have medium stability because they are closely linked with political cycles. Although the special assessment mechanism is flexible and can be adapted to variations in project costs and macroeconomic changes, its economic stability only lasts for the assessment period. Tax increment financing is stable because it is not a new tax, but a loan to developers on estimated increases in tax revenue, such as from the property or sale tax.

Sustainable Urban Transport Financing from the Sidewalk to the Subway
http://dx.doi.org/10.1596/978-1-4648-0756-5

The administrative difficulties of the instruments are related to their high transaction costs and the institutional capacity required to coordinate various agents. Successful implementation of the instruments requires decentralization and well-functioning governance structures (Medda, 2011), as well as tools to manage the different parties involved. In addition, technical capacity is needed in terms of an updated land registry and tools to assess the different benefits created by the development of the transport system. Finally, because of the high up-front revenue potential of some of these instruments, their use can lead to potential favoritism, corruption, and abuses of government power, which means the instruments must be treated as financial opportunities to increase infrastructure capacity, but not as long-term recurrent revenue sources (Peterson 2009).

The low performance on equity by the majority of indirect benefit instruments is related to the tendency of the private sector to exploit the accessibility benefits generated by transport projects mostly in areas already economically attractive and vital. Investments by the private sector triggered by transport investment in deprived areas of the city happen less frequently. The welfare impact of investment in these areas, however, might be higher and certainly is more needed.

In general, in terms of efficiency, the indirect benefit mechanisms are not very good for sending messages about the real costs associated with the use of infrastructure; hence, efficiency could only be achieved under specific conditions such as articulated densification in the vicinity of public mass transport projects (Transit Oriented Development). This, however, is not often the case as many of the mechanisms are commonly used to develop roads for mixed traffic.

Some global examples of the use of these financial instruments—joint development, tax increment financing, and betterment levies, among others—include the following:

- The city of Istanbul, Turkey, used a Joint Development mechanism for a public land sale to finance the constructions of repair centers for its metro system. In Cape Town, South Africa, the transportation agency Transnet sold public-owned land (Victoria and Albert waterfront property) to raise US$1 billion for capital investments in port and freight rail (Peterson 2009).
- Tax Increment Financing is widely used in the United States and regional areas such as Greater Manchester in the United Kingdom to generate funding for transport and urban projects that have positive impacts on adjacent areas. Examples include subway construction projects in Chicago, including the redevelopment of its Morgan Street station (US$40 million) (SDG 2010), the Randolph/Washington station (US$13.5 million), and the Lake/Wells station on the Dearborn subway line (US$1,200,000), as well as a segment for Portland's Central City Streetcar that passes through the South Park Blocks (US$7.5 million) (Casella 2002).
- In Aguas Claras, Brazil, the anticipated land purchase by federal district authorities of land to be developed for the construction of an underground line and

the subsequent sale of individual land ready to be urbanized resulted in revenue that accounted for 85 percent of the total capital investment for the underground infrastructure (CODATU 2009).

- In Germany, for capital investments, 90 percent of the cost of all roads of new development areas (including sidewalks) is covered by the developer and only 10 percent is covered by the municipal road owner. Road maintenance is generally the responsibility of the municipal road owner, while the responsibility for the rehabilitation and maintenance of sidewalks and cycle lanes is shared (with different degrees of responsibility) depending on the type of project (Sakamoto and Belka 2010).

- In Colombia, betterment levies have traditionally been used to recapture the value created by certain projects. To make the mechanism more viable and address difficulties with assessing the created value, Bogota has transformed the levy into a more general infrastructure-related tax (Peterson 2009), using the revenue to finance a package of public investments that includes street improvements and overpass construction. The financial instrument collected US$1 billion between 1997 and 2007.

Advertising and employer contributions are different from the other indirect benefit instruments in that they are not related to land or property values. The instruments both have good performance on stability and, when correctly managed, can provide recurrent funding for specific elements of the transport system. Examples of successful advertising programs are those on the *Velib* bicycle rental system in Paris (Sakamoto and Belka, 2010) and advertising on bus shelters in London. For London, advertisement revenue covers all capital and maintenance expenditures of the city's 19,000 bus shelters (Weston 2013). In France, employer contributions in the form of the *Versement Transport*, which is voluntary but strongly encouraged by local authorities, are very important for financing both capital (in particular metro and light rail infrastructure) and operation costs of cities' transport systems (Sakamoto and Belka, 2010). In Brazil, the *Vale Transporte* brings stable revenue; the instrument has been used for years as a demand subsidy for employees whose transport costs exceed 6 percent of their salary. For other attributes, however, performance is at a medium level because of the instrument's limited impact (it is only available for formal employment) and problems with its use as money on the black market (CODATU 2009).

Notes

1. The methodology for analyzing the financing instruments is based on (Sakamoto and Belka 2010), combined with elements from relevant literature and the authors' own experience; definitions of the attributes are widely based on (Binsted et al. 2010) and (Mikesell 2003) as cited by (Junge and Levinson 2012), and (Lari et al. 2009).

2. See (Peterson 2009).

Sustainable Urban Transport Financing from the Sidewalk to the Subway
http://dx.doi.org/10.1596/978-1-4648-0756-5

3. In theory, federal funding is linked to state cofunding of 20 percent of the cost, although in reality the states and local governments contribute more than 50 percent of the cost of transit projects.

4. See (Lefevre, Leipziger, and Raifman 2014) and (Kopp, A., R. Block, and A. Iimi 2012) for evidence on how small carbon financing contributes to transport financing.

5. The transfer of funds to other levels of government requires mechanisms to channel the funding in a way that it does not create distortions in the allocation of resources for different modes or weaken the incentives for efficient operations in each mode. Direct subsidy of bus operations, one of the most common forms of governmental transfer, fails on both accounts.

6. Considerable evidence exists, even in relatively poor countries such as the Kyrgyz Republic, that the poor are willing to pay more for a service that is better than the one provided at existing, controlled fares. In an extreme scenario, the poor would receive no benefits at all from the setting of very low fares if that causes supply to disappear altogether.

7. In fact, one of the important lessons and recommendations from the Transantiago experience in Santiago is that the transformation of the transport system toward higher-quality services cannot be designed to be self-financed (Gómez-Lobo and Briones 2012). Operational self-sustainability constrains will create an incentive for abusing occupation in large buses to increase revenues, creating a vicious cycle of quality of service deterioration. This highlights the tension associated with trying to simultaneously address two contradictory objectives such as providing good-quality transport and reducing costs (Figueroa 2013).

8. http://www.comune.milano.it/portale.

CHAPTER 4

From the Sidewalk to the Subway: Comprehensive and Sustainable Urban Transport Financing

Combining Instruments to Finance Transport Investments

The best financing for a specific transport investment will—of course—always depend on the specific investment project, the local context, stakeholders, and the required funding periodicity. Moreover, because of the different characteristics of the financing instruments, the large amounts of funding required, and the periodicity of expenditures, combining instruments will work best to provide comprehensive financing for all parts of a transport investment project, including capital, maintenance, and operations. Building on the assessment of individual financing instruments (presented in part 2) and the summarized findings in chapter 3, this section highlights some of the common combinations of instruments that can be used to cover those expenses for investments as varied as sidewalk renovations, road maintenance, and subway construction.

First, an analysis of the current use of financial instruments for transport projects further reinforces the finding that certain types or combinations of instruments can constitute successful financing schemes (figure 4.1). The table shows how mostly integrated and hierarchical public transport systems and rail and bus networks are usually financed by a variety of financing instruments. Other transport components, such as nonmotorized transport and roads, are mainly funded by one or two financing mechanisms, typically even in the same category.

Second, an overview of the 24 types of financing instruments in figure 4.2 illustrates how well each instrument can support different elements of the overall urban transport system. For analytical purposes, the transport system is divided into seven elements that require financing: (i) urban highways (representing capital costs); (ii) public transport and nonmotorized transport facilities

Figure 4.1 Use of Financing Instruments for Capital, Operations, and Maintenance Costs by Urban Transport Mode

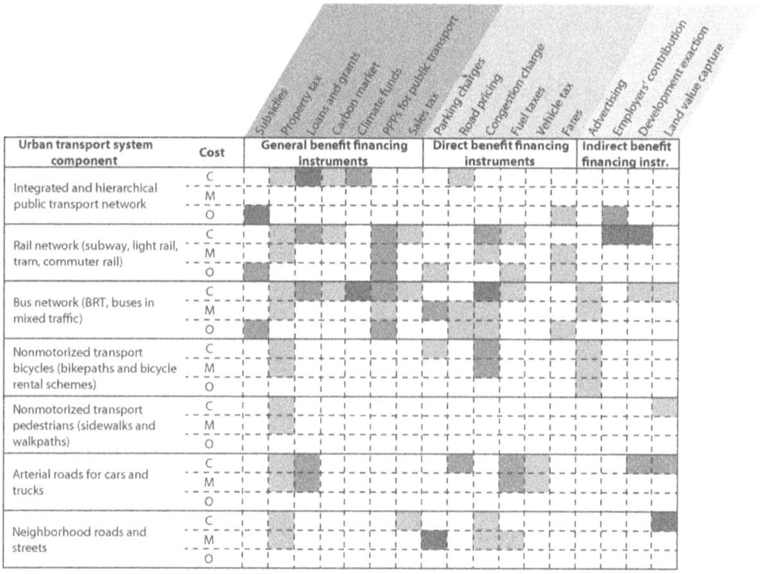

Column headers (diagonal): Subsidies; Property tax; Loans and grants; Carbon market; Climate funds; PPPs for public transport; Sales tax; Parking charges; Road pricing; Congestion charge; Fuel taxes; Vehicle tax; Fares; Advertising; Employers' contribution; Development exaction; Land value capture

Urban transport system component	Cost	General benefit financing instruments			Direct benefit financing instruments		Indirect benefit financing instr.
Integrated and hierarchical public transport network	C / M / O						
Rail network (subway, light rail, tram, commuter rail)	C / M / O						
Bus network (BRT, buses in mixed traffic)	C / M / O						
Nonmotorized transport bicycles (bikepaths and bicycle rental schemes)	C / M / O						
Nonmotorized transport pedestrians (sidewalks and walkpaths)	C / M / O						
Arterial roads for cars and trucks	C / M / O						
Neighborhood roads and streets	C / M / O						

Source: World Bank.
Note: C=capital; M=maintenance; O=operation; the darker the color of the blocks, the more the instrument was used for that purpose within the observed examples. BRT = Bus Rapid Transit.

including sidewalks (capital and operation costs); (iii) institutions that manage and operate the system (operation costs); (iv) traffic management, including intelligent transport systems (ITS) to improve traffic performance on the road network (operation); (v) technology to improve system performance, such as electronic payment systems and fleet management control systems for hierarchical integrated transport systems; (vi) education and enforcement (operation); and (vii) maintenance of existing transport infrastructure (maintenance). Maintenance is considered separately because of its large cost and critical importance to the successful performance of the system (see also figure 1.1), while the operational costs of cars are not included as they are paid for by car owners.

The figure illustrates that among the general benefit instruments both the property tax and loans and grants emerge as instruments that can finance the broadest range of transport investments. The figure further illustrates how the direct benefit instruments in particular are well suited to finance different elements of the finance system, validating a conclusion reached long ago in literature that users should pay for the costs of services they enjoy, even if instruments sometimes are politically difficult to implement. Finally, despite high administrative costs, indirect benefit instruments also can help finance elements of the system, in particular initial capital investments for road infrastructure, civil works, and public transport. Because of their high administrative costs, these instruments should only be used when expected revenue far exceeds transaction costs.

Figure 4.2   Use of Financing Instruments for Different Elements of the Urban Transport System

General
Public Transport Subsidies
Property Tax
Loans and Grants
Carbon Market
Global Environment Facility
Clean Technology Fund
PPPs for Public Transport

Direct
Parking Charges
Road Pricing
Congestion Charges
Fuel Taxes/Surcharges
Vehicle Taxation
Farebox Revenue
PPPs for Urban Roads

Indirect
Advertising
Employers Contribution
Betterment Levies
Tax Increment Financing
Special Assessment
Transportation Utility Fees
Development Impact Fee
Negotiated Exactions
Joint Development (PPP)
Air Rights

⊟ Urban highways   ░ Notmotorized and public transport
▥ Institutions   ☐ Traffic management and ITS
▨ Education and enforcement   ▨ Technology
■ Maintenance

Source: CODATU 2009; Sakamoto and Belka 2010; Zhao, Das, and Larson 2012.
Note: PPP = public–private partnership.

Moving Forward: Integrated Transport Planning, Wise Investments, and the Role for Public Subsidies

Overall, the analysis, based on a framework that integrates the concepts of "Who Benefits Pays" and wise investments, leads to several general recommendations for the design of urban transport and its financing schemes:

- Link urban transport planning and operations with urban planning. The analysis supports the concept—already widely agreed in literature—that urban transport planning and operations should be an integral part of a city's urban strategy (Gwilliam 2002). Only when part of a larger strategy can individual

Sustainable Urban Transport Financing from the Sidewalk to the Subway
http://dx.doi.org/10.1596/978-1-4648-0756-5

investments be designed to increase benefit and revenue and limit future costs (for example, in terms of curbing sprawl and promoting denser development with good design) (Cervero 1997).

- Combine revenue sources. Urban transport systems are large and complex, and a combination of financing instruments is needed to ensure financial sustainability. The analysis of instruments in this book can provide the basis for city assessments of what combinations of instruments might be most appropriate for specific investments considering their benefits, costs, and trade-offs in terms of financial and transport sustainability.

- Consider the effect of instruments on transport demand. Not only the choice of transport investment but also the choice of instrument will affect the use and demand for transport systems in a city. In addition, instruments can be used to improve the environmental sustainability of transport options, for example by encouraging service suppliers to find technological alternatives. Rather than selecting instruments only to provide the funding for an investments, the choice of instruments can be seen as a part of the overall transport system strategy. Part 2 provides a detailed description and analysis of each instrument.

- Ensure appropriate use of public subsidies. As discussed in chapter 3, it is important, under appropriate conditions, to use public subsidies to support investment in transport projects that provide overall benefits for society and guarantee accessibility through high-quality public transport services, while avoiding implicit subsidies—such as those for gasoline and diesel (Kopp, A., R. Block, and A. Iimi 2012)—that support the inefficiencies of private agents (users, operators, and companies). Although more subsidies from the public sector might be required, direct and indirect beneficiaries should contribute with amounts proportionate to their benefit share. To ensure an appropriate use of public subsidies, subsidies should be coupled with regulations and managing and monitoring tools, such as contract and quality performance indicators, to guarantee that subsidies are not compensating private sector's inefficiencies but are used to invest in high-quality sustainable public transport for society as a whole.

- Allow cities financial autonomy and capacity. Cities must have the autonomy and capacity to design their financial schemes according to their investment responsibilities. In this context, a property tax can be an important tool as it is a cost-effective way to raise critical revenue to cover the capital, maintenance, and operation costs for elements of the transport system, such as, for example, neighborhood roads and sidewalks, that benefit the population in general. As their benefits are general, it is generally not economically feasible to charge for their use.[1]

- Allow a role for national governments. When local instruments, such as the property tax, are not sufficient to cover capital investments, cities can also access loans from different sources. The analysis clearly shows—thanks to the benefit principle—that in this case national governments also must play a role, if the benefits of having a good urban transport system go beyond the city itself. That is why countries such as the United Kingdom, the United States, Germany, France, Mexico, Brazil, China, and Colombia all have programs to finance urban transport infrastructure, specifically mass transit improvements. In addition, international funding can play a strong role in light of climate change and the need to invest in projects that contribute to the global benefit of reducing emissions from the transport sector. For urban highways, national programs rarely support investments, and this is validated by the analysis. The benefits of urban highways are more concentrated, and users should pay for a large share or even all the capital costs. Likewise, users should cover the associated operation and maintenance expenses of urban roads.

- Understand the need for a gradual introduction of user charges. The analysis suggests that the political acceptability of user charges is low. To break this stalemate, a gradual introduction of user charges has to be considered, as well as appropriate combinations with other instruments and a provision of good public transport services as alternative to private car use. Fuel taxes earmarked for use in the transport system are a good way to begin. Fuel taxes reflect use and can be a stable source, with low administrative costs; they also promote efficiency and equity and help achieve environmental goals. Next, parking fees could be introduced, followed by congestion pricing or other measures.

- Consider land value–based financing instruments. Land value–based financing instruments are a great way to attract resources from the private sector and increase overall revenue for the system. These instruments are especially useful to finance important capital investment to increase the capacity of the transport system. Nonetheless, careful consideration has to be given to the estimation of the added value and created benefits and to their long-term use as a recurrent financing source, as individuals might be reluctant to pay twice for the same perceived benefit.

Note

1. The Singapore Land Transport Authority is beginning to assess the possibility of charging for car use the moment a car enters a neighborhood road. The system will expand Singapore's famous Electronic Road Pricing system, which currently charges only in the most congested area of the city.

CHAPTER 5

Conclusion

The proposed analytical framework presents an innovative way to analyze financing instruments and help design comprehensive urban transport financing schemes. Based on a "Who Benefits Pays" principle and focusing on wise investments, the framework can help cities fund urgent urban transport investments, identify who should pay for them, and help reduce the future financing gap for transport.

Application of the framework to 24 financing instruments identified some of the key strengths and weaknesses across the different categories of general, direct, and indirect benefit instruments. In addition, the analysis highlighted broader issues related to urban transport financing schemes, key among which is the need—and opportunity—to combine appropriate instruments and revenue sources to finance different modes as part of sustainable integrated transport systems.

Overall, the findings of the analysis support that cities must aim to achieve financial sustainability for their urban transport systems by combining both innovative multitier financing and wiser investments. Innovative financing refers to the revenue side, which can increase if different financial instruments are combined and managed effectively. Wiser investments, associated with the expenditure side, means strategically choosing to develop cost-effective projects that contribute to solving short-term difficulties while working to achieve long-term transport sustainability goals. More specifically, the revenue-side perspective acknowledges that the observed underfinancing of the transport sector stems from the existing price distortions that have tacitly contributed to the subsidizing of certain mode inefficiencies, particularly those of the private car. Therefore, an ideal financing strategy should aim at setting financial instruments at prices that charge users for the total costs of using a given infrastructure or transport service; this pricing will correct market distortions, improve user behavior, and increase revenue to a level equal to or above expenditures.

Financial and transport sustainability both can be supported through appropriate combinations of complementary instruments in terms of, for example, revenue periodicity and beneficiaries. For capital investments, a combination of grants and loans from funding agencies combined with investments through public–private partnerships could finance large projects that benefit society. The property tax also emerges as a key financing instrument of capital, operations, and maintenance. Although individual project circumstances will vary, the framework guides the assessment of revenue options and helps cities use instruments strategically to not only fund needed transport investment but also actually achieve their larger sustainable urban transport and development objectives.

In sum, by choosing the most appropriate sets of financing instruments and focusing on wise investments, cities can design comprehensive financing for all types of urban transport projects, using multilevel innovative revenue sources that promote efficient pricing schemes, increase overall revenue, strengthen sustainable transport, and cover capital investments, operation, and maintenance for the sidewalk to the subway.

PART 2

Financing Instruments

CHAPTER 6

General Benefit Instruments

General benefit instruments are financial instruments for which the beneficiary and funder is the general public (see also chapter 2). Instruments include public transport subsidies, property taxes, and national and international grants and loans. Section "Public Transport Subsidies, Property Taxes, and National and International Grants and Loans" presents the analysis findings for those three types of instruments.[1] Climate-related financial instruments are discussed in more detail in section "Climate-Related Financing Instruments."

Public Transport Subsidies, Property Taxes, and National and International Grants and Loans

Tables 6.1, 6.2, and 6.3[2] present the financial and transport sustainability of public transport subsidies, property taxes, and national and international grants and loans.

Table 6.1 Framework Analysis Results for Public Transport Subsidies

General characteristics	
Financing instrument	Public transport subsidies
Benefit	General tax-base growth; accessibility and economic growth
Beneficiary/funder	General public
Level of government	Local and national
Periodicity	Recurrent
Type of expense	Maintenance and operation
Financial sustainability	
Stability	**Low.** Public transport subsidies depend on overall financial health as they commonly derive from the general tax budget or from transfers from the national government to specific funds or programs (Sakamoto and Belka 2010) of a lower governmental level (state, regional, or local). They can also come from local transport authorities between modes. Subsidies can vary over time due to economic cycles or political changes and shifting priorities.

table continues next page

Table 6.1 Framework Analysis Results for Public Transport Subsidies *(continued)*

Political and public acceptability	**High**. Subsidies to public transport are generally highly accepted by the general public and also have high political acceptability. Although higher taxes can have a negative connotation, they can be overlooked if the perceived benefits of the increase in accessibility are clear and significant.
Convenience and administrative ease	**Medium**. Although transport authorities and transport funds can facilitate management of subsidy resources, defining adequate levels of funding and effectively allocating the funds to the beneficiaries requires coordination among various entities, as well as accounting transparency. In general, public authorities may link operational payments or subsidy compensation to the fulfilment of productivity criteria based on a service agreement, laying down the rights and obligations of operators, whether public or private.

Transport sustainability

Efficiency	**Medium**. Subsidies for public transport can be for capital investments or operations and maintenance. In general, subsidies are needed to at least cover capital costs because of the large lump sums required, for example, to build a metro or bus rapid transit line. While cities grow incrementally, they need lump-sum investments for transport infrastructure. In contrast, for operations and maintenance—as well as some capital costs such as those for fleet, efficient pricing should lead to covering costs (Gomez-Ibanez 1999). The review in this book, however, found that subsidies for operation and maintenance are frequently used, often as a subsidy to the provider of the service ("supply-side subsidies"). Supply-side subsidies can have negative incentives and could be used to mostly cover operators' inefficiencies (Gwilliam 2002). If subsidies must be used, fares should be set to cover as much of the costs as possible, and subsidies should go to the users, as "demand-based subsidies." Demand-based subsidies allow targeting the neediest in society while having those with enough income pay for the service (Estupinan et al. 2007). Therefore, subsidies for public transport are recommended to be used either for capital costs or--if used for operating costs--for the "demand side" only.
Equity	**High**. Even though the modal distribution (low motorization rates) in developing cities often allows a self-sustainable operation of transport systems, lower-income populations (for whom transport expenses represent an important proportion of their income) face affordability issues that have to be addressed through demand-side subsidies to prevent social exclusion. Alternatively, in many cities, especially in developed countries, public transport subsidies are required to compensate for the low patronage in public transport caused by high usage of private cars (due to implicit subsidies).
Environmental impact	**Medium**. As subsidies to public transport incentivize the use of this mode, they help reduce transport-related emissions due to a modal shift. However, subsidies for fuel, often given to operators, have a negative environmental impact as they prevent service providers from accounting for the real cost of their fuel consumption and do not incentivize them to find more efficient technologies or operation practices (that is, preventive maintenance and ecodriving training).

table continues next page

Table 6.1 **Framework Analysis Results for Public Transport Subsidies** *(continued)*

Other considerations	
Associated risks	Subsidies must be treated carefully as they go against the user-pays principle and seem to create distortions. They should therefore be coupled with regulations to guarantee the subsidies are not used to compensate private sector's inefficiencies. For example, subsidies for fuel are, in a way, subsidies to the private sector, creating a distortion regarding the cost of providing the service. To incentivize better industrial practices, as well as efficiency and innovation for reducing costs, fuel subsidies should be removed and instead given directly to users or to specific services that are unprofitable but have a high social impact. Similarly, not charging private vehicles for the real social costs of their use is an implicit subsidy that results in inefficient travel decisions and an "overconsumption" of car use and infrastructure.
	A better approach for thinking about subsidies could be to treat them as funding to the demand side to guarantee affordability and inclusion of the entire population or, as in the case of London, Paris, Barcelona, or Santiago de Chile, as public investment in high-quality integrated transport systems.
Main sources	(CODATU 2009), (Binsted et al. 2010), (Sakamoto and Belka 2010)

Table 6.2 **Framework Analysis Results for Property Taxes**

General characteristics	
Financing instrument	Property taxes
Benefit	General tax-base growth as a consequence of increases in property values due to general improvements in the city
Beneficiary/funder	General public
Level of government	Local and national
Periodicity	Recurrent
Type of expense	Capital, maintenance, and operation
Financial sustainability	
Stability	**High.** Usually based on the value of the property (in fewer cases on the size), property taxes have a wide tax base that is relatively constant in the medium term. Rates are also relatively stable and can be adjusted annually for inflation, supporting long-term planning. Property taxes can therefore yield important revenues and are frequently one of the main sources of funding for cities.
Political and public acceptability	**Medium.** Public and political acceptance increases when the charging mechanism is clear and perceived as evenly distributed.
Convenience and administrative ease	**Medium.** Local government capacity for collecting the tax depends on the quality and accuracy of its cadaster to provide an updated and detailed database on properties (World Bank 2013). Although it can cost considerable time and resources to construct such a database, once established, the collection and management costs are low, given that all properties in the city are charged. It is important that compliance rates are high so that collected revenue does not have to be used to enforce payment.

table continues next page

Sustainable Urban Transport Financing from the Sidewalk to the Subway
http://dx.doi.org/10.1596/978-1-4648-0756-5

Table 6.2 Framework Analysis Results for Property Taxes *(continued)*

Transport sustainability	
Efficiency	**Low**. The benefits received by the property owners are not necessarily related to a specific transport project. However, development of public transport projects or investment in road infrastructure to improve accessibility and the overall quality of life in the city should be reflected to a certain extent in the value of the property.
Equity	**Medium**. The tax promotes equity as it charges higher taxes to those who have properties with higher values. Since the funding is then reinvested around the city in different projects, the tax has a progressive distributive effect.
Environmental impact	**Low**. The tax does not send any direct message to citizens regarding travel behavior related to fuel consumption or emissions. Nonetheless, if invested, for example, in improving local roads, it could improve operating conditions and lead to more efficient driving.
Other considerations	
Associated risks	Property taxes are typically used to finance local road networks, and it seems that particularly in very large regions if localities are small enough, locals are best placed to value and pay for such networks. For example, in a region like the Washington, DC larger metropolitan area (in the United States), property taxes would be a fairly efficient way of paying for networks of local access roads in areas such as Frederick, Bethesda, or Loudon (just outside the district and in the state of Maryland), given that (as per (Tiebout 1956)) residents have the option of moving to the locality that provides them with the best combination of local property taxes and services. The mainstay of local government revenue systems is the property tax, but this remains underutilized with an effective rate against GDP at about half the international average for developing countries (Mathur, Thakur, and Rajadhyaksha 2009). Property taxes need to be properly administered to be effective. The Indian property tax could be administered better, for example. A survey of the property tax practice in the 36 largest urban local governments, carried out by Mathur (Mathur, Thakur, and Rajadhyaksha 2009) revealed that 44 percent of all parcels are excluded from the tax net, properties are assessed at about 30 percent of market value, and the average collection rate is about 40 percent.
Main sources	(Zegras 2006), (Bahl, Linn, and Wetzel 2013), (Farvacque-Vitkovic and Kopanyi 2014)

Table 6.3 Framework Analysis Results for National and International Loans and Grants

General characteristics	
Financing instrument	Loans and grants from national and international organizations, private organizations (such as commercial banks), or foreign sources (such as governments of industrialized countries, either bilaterally or through multilateral institutions such as the World Bank.)
Benefit	General benefit
Beneficiary/funder	General public
Level of government	National and local
Type of expense	Capital and maintenance

table continues next page

Table 6.3 Framework Analysis Results for National and International Loans and Grants *(continued)*

Periodicity	Up front and recurrent
Financial sustainability	
Stability	**High**. Loans and grants are stable and usually associated with funding programs or legislation frameworks. Grants often do not require future repayment but a fulfillment of certain conditions, such as specific levels of contributions by the local government or private sector. Financial aid from funding agencies gives credibility to a project and can help attract other sources of financing, thus improving the overall stability of the project.
Political and public acceptability	**High**. Funding agencies have provided billions of dollars for the development of road infrastructure[a] and, in recent years, specific public transport projects. These loans and grants are received by the public as promoters of development. In particular when funding is coming from multilateral institutions such as the World Bank, the financial aid is supported by institutional and regulatory advice and support to ensure the required institutional capabilities for successful project implementation are also acquired.
Convenience and administrative ease	**Medium**. Loans and grants are often managed at a national level, although some countries have schemes to also allow local or transport authorities to apply for loans, usually under stricter conditions.[b] Although, in general, coordination among government levels and agencies is difficult and increases transaction costs, the planning, institutional, and evaluation frameworks developed as part of the funding process[c] can significantly reduce any difficulties stemming from the involvement of a large number of agents.
Transport sustainability	
Efficiency	**High**. Loans provided by national or international public entities allow a government access to large amounts of capital that otherwise would not be available and at interest rates below those typical in the private market. Project development based on these long-term low interest rates may represent millions in financial savings for the authority. Moreover, when used to develop sustainable transport projects, the loans also represent economic savings by reducing future social, economic, and environmental costs of unsustainable transport and land use patterns.
Equity	**High**. Project investments in the form of loans or grants generally benefit the majority of the population. In addition, they can create generational equity, as lower interest rates and financial and economic savings guarantee more resources are available for future generations. Finally, improving the technical and institutional capacities at different government levels facilitates future development of sustainable transport projects.
Environmental impact	**High**. Within the framework of transport sustainability, loans and grants have been typically allocated to projects that give priority to public transport and nonmotorized modes, having a direct impact on emissions reductions.

table continues next page

Sustainable Urban Transport Financing from the Sidewalk to the Subway
http://dx.doi.org/10.1596/978-1-4648-0756-5

Table 6.3 Framework Analysis Results for National and International Loans and Grantss *(continued)*

Other considerations	
Associated risks	Although in some countries, such as Germany, France, the United States, and the United Kingdom, funding is available for operation costs of different modes (that is, fuel and energy costs, administrative expenses, and operational and maintenance staff salaries), national loans and grants mostly support capital costs. In countries such as India, Mexico, and other countries in Latin America, operation is self-financed from fees or fares and through public–private partnerships. However, these characteristics, combined with a social pressure to keep fares low, have threatened the quality of services and maintenance of the system (Sakamoto and Belka 2010).
Main sources	(Sakamoto and Belka 2010), (CODATU 2009), (Gwilliam 2000), (Medda 2011), (Binsted et al. 2010), (Sastre-González 2012)

a. Several authors, such as (Sakamoto and Belka 2010), (CODATU 2009), (Gwilliam 2000), (Medda 2011), highlighted how past trends of loans and grants by multilateral institutions such as the World Bank were focused more on road infrastructure provision than on public transport provision, due mainly to the fact that higher risk were associated with public modes. However, in light of sustainable development and the need to apply sustainability principles in all sectors, during the last couple of decades the focus has been shifting and now it has been completely given to promoting sustainable transport projects and reducing emissions from the sector.
b. Prudential Borrowing for Local grant in the United Kingdom gives the option to get loans directly from the market or through the Public Works Loan Board (Sakamoto and Belka 2010).
c. This includes clarity regarding the agency in charge (regional, municipal, local), the eligibility criteria and main conditions for allocation (such as city size and characteristic of competitive bidding processes on the basis of a specific need or scheme), and characteristic of the awarded funding (for example, loan or grant, maximum amount, and availability (perhaps only on a one-off basis) (Sakamoto and Belka 2010).

Climate-Related Financing Instruments

Climate financing includes several types of instruments, yet the amount of funding provided by these instruments is considered to be relatively low (Binsted et al. 2010, and Lefevre, Leipziger, and Raifman 2014) compared to other more traditional instruments. Climate financing instruments are not meant to stand on their own but to be part of a funding strategy in which only the incremental cost associated with the mitigation of environmental impact is financed through these mechanisms. Climate financing instruments are versatile in terms of the financing sources (public or private) and the type of sectors and projects (technology transfers, capacity building, planning, infrastructure, operation and management) they can finance. Nonetheless, each climate financing instrument has very specific eligibility criteria, usually related to the need to quantify the investment's impact on climate change mitigation (ensuring impacts are measurable, reportable, and verifiable). Figure 6.1 presents an overview of the main climate financing instruments.

Tables 6.4, 6.5, and 6.6 provide more detail on the three main climate finance instruments used for transport projects. The first two (Global Environment Facility and the Clean Technology Fund) are multilateral and bilateral mechanisms, while the Clean Development Mechanism (CDM) is associated with the carbon market.

Figure 6.1 Overview of Climate Financing Instruments

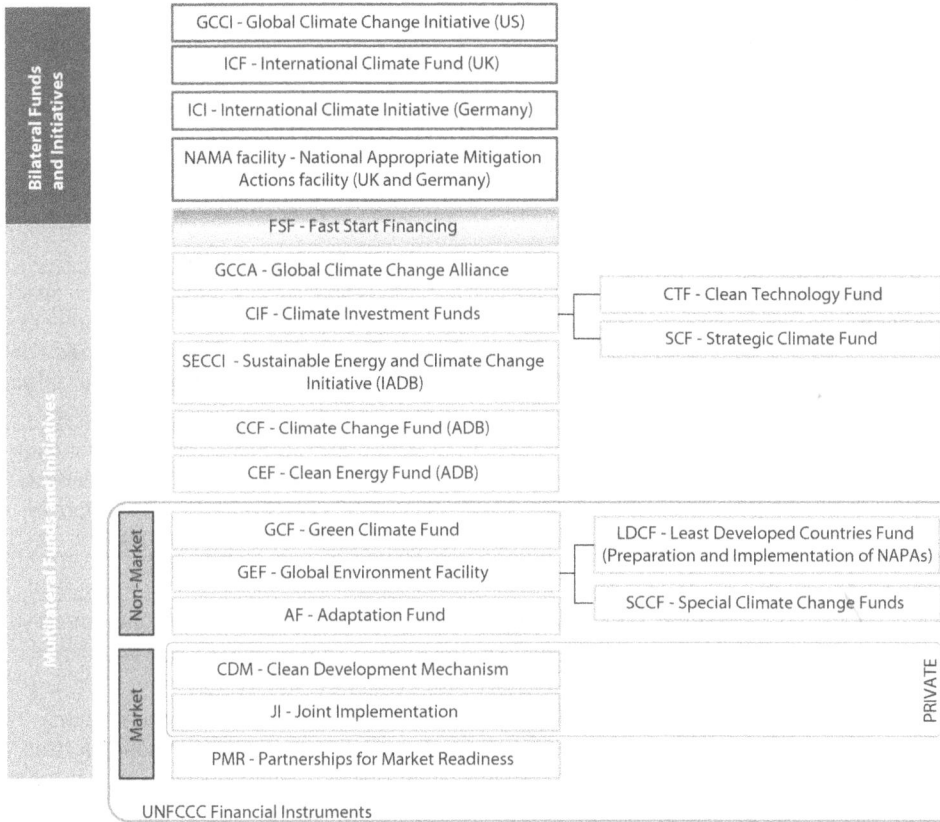

Source: Authors based on Binsted et al. 2010; Nakhooda et al. 2012.
Note: UNFCCC = United Nations Framework Convention on Climate Change. NAPAs = National adaptation programmes of action. IADB = Inter American Development Bank. ADB = Asian Development Bank.

Table 6.4 Framework Analysis Results for the Global Environment Facility (GEF)

General characteristics	
Financing instrument	Global Environment Facility (GEF)
Benefit	Greenhouse gas emission reduction
Beneficiary/funder	General public
Level of government	International and national
Type of expense	Capital and operation
Periodicity	Up front and recurrent

table continues next page

Table 6.4 Framework Analysis Results for the Global Environment Facility (GEF) *(continued)*

Financial sustainability	
Stability	**Low**. GEF provides loans and grants to promote innovative projects and programs that contribute to the protection of the global environment through a transformation of the business as usual scenario. GEF funding needs to address national priorities and programs and be consistent with focal strategies. The loans and grants, however, only finance the incremental costs of measures to achieve environmental benefits, which means this instrument's availability depends on other mechanisms being in place.
Political and public acceptability	**Medium**. Support from GEF not only is financial but also comprises capacity building and technology transfers, which increases the instrument's acceptability. GEF projects seek to address broader negative impacts, requiring projects to be comprehensive and integrated interventions. This can have different effects on acceptability, depending on the context.
Convenience and administrative ease	**Medium**. GEF-supported projects usually need additional cofunding. Although GEF has supported several sustainable transport-related projects in developing countries, the complexity of the project approval process (including the requirements for emissions accounting) has been a barrier to uptake.
Transport sustainability	
Efficiency	**Medium**. Although the instrument can be used to finance comprehensive, integrated interventions, the main focus is minimizing environmental externalities.
Equity	**Medium**. The instrument does not have a clear impact on equity factors. In general, however, projects that prioritize investment in nonmotorized modes have a positive impact on lower-income populations as they are the main users of those modes in developing cities.
Environmental impact	**High**. The instrument's main focus is delivering quantifiable and tangible environmental benefits.
Other considerations	
Associated risks	–
Main sources	Binsted et al. 2010; Sakamoto and Belka 2010

Table 6.5 Framework Analysis Results for the Clean Technology Fund

General characteristics	
Financing instrument	Clean Technology Fund (CTF)
Benefit	Greenhouse gas emission reduction
Beneficiary/funder	General public
Level of government	International, national, and regional
Type of expense	Capital and operation
Periodicity	Up front and recurrent

table continues next page

Table 6.5 Framework Analysis Results for the Clean Technology Fund *(continued)*

Financial sustainability	
Stability	**Medium**. The instrument provides a broad multisectorial programmatic approach to funding clean technology projects. The fund provides limited grants and concessional loans, partial risk guarantees, or risk mitigation instruments and funding for initiatives to strengthen climate resilience. Most interventions seeking this type of climate funding, however, rely on additional funding outside the CTF.
Political and public acceptability	**Medium**. The application procedure requires the World Bank, the Regional Development Bank, and project stakeholders (government officials, civil society, and industry) to jointly prepare an Investment Plan to describe how the financing will be used and how it can contribute to existing strategies. The process of defining a joint Investment Plan facilitates, to some extent, the political acceptability.
Convenience and administrative ease	**Medium**. Similar to political acceptability, the process of defining the Investment Plan helps define which agents will be involved and coordination strategies.
Transport sustainability	
Efficiency	**Medium**. Funding is mostly directed at minimizing environmental externalities.
Equity	**Medium**. Although projects do not specifically address equity, in general, projects that prioritize investment in nonmotorized modes have a positive impact on lower-income populations, as they are the main users of those modes in developing cities.
Environmental impact	**High**. CTF specifically focuses on delivering measurable emission reductions and achieving environmental benefits.
Other considerations	
Associated risks	–
Main sources	Kopp, A., R. Block, and A. Iimi 2012; Binsted et al. 2010

Table 6.6 Framework Analysis Results for the Clean Development Mechanism

General characteristics	
Financing instrument	Carbon Market–Clean Development Mechanism (CDM)
Benefit	Greenhouse gas emission reduction
Beneficiary/funder	General public (global)
Level of government	International and national
Type of expense	Capital and operation
Periodicity	Up front and recurrent

table continues next page

Table 6.6 Framework Analysis Results for the Clean Development Mechanism *(continued)*

Financial sustainability

Stability	**Low**. Introduced by the Kyoto Protocol in 2005, Clean Development Mechanism (CDM) has become one of the main instruments for funding climate change mitigation projects in developing countries.[a] The stability of the instrument depends on the possibility of accurately measuring emission reductions that can be directly linked to a specific activity. In that case, carbon emission reduction (CERs) credits can be traded on the carbon market.
Political and public acceptability	**High**. Funding from external sources at presumably no cost has high political and public acceptability.
Convenience and administrative ease	**Low**. CDM funding is based on the amount of greenhouse gas emission reductions achieved by the transport projects. Procedures to certify CERs are genuine and very strict.

Transport sustainability

Efficiency	**Medium**. CDM is a market-based instrument that allows industrialized countries with an international obligation to meet greenhouse reduction targets to invest in projects in developing countries to achieve their targets there at a lower cost. From the transport system's perspective, this means that those directly benefitting from the project are not paying for it.
Equity	**Medium**. On a global level, a distributive effect from industrialized (higher-income) countries to developing countries is occurring. Developing countries benefit by receiving financing for better infrastructure and cleaner technologies.
Environmental impact	**High**. The funding is specifically designed to achieve objectives in this area. Cleaner and more environmentally efficient technologies such as public and nonmotorized transport are prioritized.

Other considerations

Associated risks	The main difficulties associated with the mechanism have been developing the methodologies and data collection to measure, report, and verify reductions. Consequently, the actual application of CDM in the transport sector has been very limited, with only two projects in operation (Bogota's BRT and New Delhi's metro using regenerating breaking technology).
Main sources	Sakamoto and Belka 2010; Binsted et al. 2010

a. As of 2010, 4,926 CDM projects had been submitted for approbation to the CDM executive board (Sakamoto and Belka 2010).

Notes

1. As described in chapter 3, the methodology for analyzing the financing instruments in this and subsequent sections is based on (Sakamoto and Belka 2010) combined with elements from relevant literature and the authors' own experience; definitions of the attributes are widely based on (Binsted et al. 2010) and Mikesell (2003) as cited by (Junge and Levinson 2012) and (Lari et al. 2009).

2. All tables in part 2 were done by the authors.

CHAPTER 7

Direct Benefit Instruments

Direct benefit instruments are those financial instruments that directly charge specific groups for certain benefits received. The instruments discussed include parking charges (table 7.1), road pricing (table 7.2), congestion charges (table 7.3), fuel taxes and surcharges (table 7.4), vehicle taxation (table 7.5), and fare box revenue (table 7.6).

Table 7.1 Framework Analysis Results for Parking Charges

General characteristics	
Financing instrument	Parking charges
Benefit	Zone access rights
Beneficiary/funder	Users/private-vehicle drivers
Level of government	Local
Type of expense	Capital, maintenance, and operation
Periodicity	Recurrent
Financial sustainability	
Stability	**Medium**. Revenue from this source is relatively stable in the medium term as access to certain zones will always be in demand. However, the amount of resources the instrument can generate depends on the actual parking spaces that are publicly regulated, which are usually limited to on-street parking areas. Moreover, success of the measure can reduce the amount of vehicles in the area and reduce revenue levels. Revenue can be increased by extending the charges to private organizations and companies as workplace parking levies.
Political and public acceptability	**Low**. When associated with on-street parking (on spaces perceived as public spaces), acceptability of the measure is low. Similarly, when related to private parking spaces on commercial properties, opposition from the businesses can make implementation difficult,[a] even though it can be imposed through legislation. Acceptability can be increased by investing revenues locally (such as for local roads and public spaces). Measures can also be tailored to each company's situation.

table continues next page

Table 7.1 Framework Analysis Results for Parking Charges *(continued)*

Convenience and administrative ease	**Medium.** Collection and enforcement require investments in technology, labor (officers), and coordination among stakeholders and agents involved.

Transport sustainability

Efficiency	**High.** For users, the cost is directly linked to the benefit of entering a certain area by car. To encourage more sustainable behavior, parking fees should be set based on the relationship between off- and on-street parking fees and fees for hourly parking compared to a single public transport fare. Fee structure should also discourage travel during peak hours while encouraging off-peak-hour travel (for example by customers).
Equity	**High.** The instrument leads to efficient allocation of scarce public resources (such as space) in urban areas.
Environmental impact	**Medium.** The instrument reduces the amount of vehicles in a certain area and prevents speed reductions to find an available parking spot. This minimizes external costs such as mild congestion, thus decreasing travel times and pollution (Santos, Behrendt, and Teytelboym 2010).

Other considerations

Associated risks	Effective implementation of the instrument without adequate provision of substitutes for private car use (such as good-quality public transport, car sharing, teleworking, and other arrangements) might reduce overall trips to an area and threaten economic productivity.
Main sources	CODATU 2009; Sakamoto and Belka 2010; Wright 2007; Breithaupt 2004

a. People are reluctant to give up car parking spaces associated with properties, even if they do not own a car, because they perceive a property without a parking space to lose value. Stubbs (2002) and Rye and Ison (2005) argue that many private sector employers in the United Kingdom meet resistance from employees in the face of parking charges. As cited by (Santos, Behrendt, and Teytelboym 2010).

Table 7.2 Framework Analysis Results for Road Pricing

General characteristics

Financing instrument	Road pricing
Benefit	General access rights
Beneficiary/funder	Users/private-vehicle drivers
Level of government	Local
Type of expense	Capital, maintenance, and operation
Periodicity	Recurrent

Financial sustainability

Stability	**Medium.** Amount of revenue can be affected by economic cycles that reduce demand and overall motorization rates.
Political and public acceptability	**Low.** Requires good-quality information to prepare users and present benefits. Car users make decision based on out-of-pocket costs such as parking. They do not see other costs such as externalities generated by them using the car. Car users will see road pricing as an additional financial burden and oppose it.

table continues next page

Table 7.2 Framework Analysis Results for Road Pricing *(continued)*

Convenience and administrative ease	**Medium**. Charges can be made through time-dependent tolling or electronic road pricing.

Transport sustainability

Efficiency	**High**. Road pricing is a mechanism for directly charging users for the benefit of using a segment of the road. The rate can be flexible to either (i) fully cover the benefit of using a car (used at the expense of society as it imposes negative externalities under very costly conditions, such as congestion, higher emissions and noise, and scarcity of road space) or (ii) improve traffic flow on a specific road or lane by diminishing the amount of vehicles entering a certain area. The second option is more flexible in the sense that it can be differentiated for the road, time of day, and type of vehicle.
Equity	**High**. Road pricing is considered an equitable measure, especially in developing countries where private car users generally belong to higher-income populations. The measure might be progressive if the revenue collected from the charge is earmarked for public transport investments (as is the case in London) or nonmotorized infrastructure.
Environmental impact	**High**. The instrument reduces the amount of vehicles on a certain corridor at certain times, generating an overall reduction of emissions from the transport system.

Other considerations

Associated risks	Transferring road pricing revenue to public transport services is not always possible. Under private concessions, transfers to public transport services are only possible after loan repayments are completed and operation and maintenance costs are covered; under public private partnerships, transfers to public transport are only possible if stated in the contract. In addition, if nontoll alternatives are available, charges will only be paid by those willing to pay for time or convenience gains. To maintain a certain level of profitability, a certain level of demand (congestion) is needed, and tolls have to be set accordingly.
Main sources	CODATU 2009; Sakamoto and Belka 2010; Zegras 2006; DeGood 2011

Table 7.3 Framework Analysis Results for Congestion charges

General characteristics

Financing instrument	Congestion charges
Benefit	Demand based access right
Beneficiary/funder	Users/private-vehicle drivers
Level of government	Local
Type of expense	Capital, maintenance, and operation
Periodicity	Recurrent

table continues next page

Table 7.3 Framework Analysis Results for Congestion charges *(continued)*

Financial sustainability	
Stability	**Medium.** The instrument depends on the amount of vehicles traveling to a certain area, so can be affected by economic cycles, patterns related to motorization rates, and economic conditions in the area. The buoyancy of the mechanism is high in the sense that price increases might reduce the demand considerably.
Political and public acceptability	**Low.** In the early stages of planning, congestion charges might be perceived to create social exclusion, especially if the quality of available public transport is low and public transport is regarded by private-vehicle users as a noncomparable substitute in terms of quality, safety, security, comfort, and time efficiency. However, if good-quality public transport is in place, public acceptance generally improves upon implementation due to the observed gains. When the mechanism is more progressive, public acceptability is higher.
Convenience and administrative ease	**Medium.** Technology is needed to exert control and enforcement and collect payments. Because this can be expensive and lead to proportionally high operational costs, the fee has to be set carefully so that the demand level is enough to cover management costs.
Transport sustainability	
Efficiency	**High.** Charges represent an extra cost associated with the use of a vehicle in a certain area and/or a certain time. Using technology, differential rates can be used, allowing more benefits to be captured.
Equity	**High.** Similar to road pricing, congestion charging is considered an equitable measure, especially in developing countries where most private car users belong to high-income populations. The measure might be progressive if the revenue collected from the charge is earmarked for public transport investments (as in London) or in nonmotorized infrastructures and facilities, including public spaces.
Environmental impact	**High.** The measure encourages more efficient travel patterns, incentivizes modal shift, and reduces "unnecessary" trips. Fewer running vehicles also implies better operating conditions (less congestion) and fewer emissions.
Other considerations	
Associated risks	Congestion charges should, ideally, be coordinated by a transport authority, so they can be aligned with transport policies and strategies. The authority should have effective leverage associated with a direct control of revenues or the capacity to exercise indirect control by imposing regulations or setting rates. Incapacity to provide alternative modes to adequately substitute private vehicles can result in a level of social exclusion, especially for car users in middle- and lower-income groups, who cannot afford to pay the charge.
Main sources	CODATU 2009; Sakamoto and Belka 2010; Zegras 2006; DeGood 2011; Replogle 2008

Table 7.4 Framework Analysis Results for Fuel Taxes/Surcharges

General characteristics	
Financing instrument	Fuel taxes/surcharges
Benefit	Gas consumption/distance driven
Beneficiary/funder	Users/private-vehicle drivers
Level of government	Local and national
Type of expense	Capital, maintenance, and operation
Periodicity	Recurrent
Financial sustainability	
Stability	**High**. Fuel taxes are stable instruments for financing road maintenance and even, in some cases, road construction. Although fuel prices might respond to economic conditions, any demand decreases due to price increases are usually compensated by an increase in the tax base (increasing motorization). Large increases in surcharges, however, can defer people from using vehicles, resulting in less revenue.[a]
Political and public acceptability	**Low**. Although relatively "hidden" within the fuel price, fuel taxes generally prevent fuel prices from changing substantially, even when international prices do. This is not well received by users.
Convenience and administrative ease	**High**. Fuel taxes are a popular mechanism to increase revenues, given that their implementation, enforcement, and administration are relatively easy.
Transport sustainability	
Efficiency	**High**. The cost of fuel taxes are borne directly by users proportionally to the amount of fuel consumed, which is a good indicator of their road usage and distance travelled.
Equity	**High**. Revenue from fuel taxes or surcharges can be earmarked, for example, for public transport projects. In that case, the taxes have a redistributive effect because the taxes are paid mainly by high-income populations owning private cars, while public transport is primarily used by medium- and low-income populations.
Environmental impact	**High**. Revenue from fuel taxes increases with the amount of fuel consumed, directly reflecting the environmental cost of using a motorized vehicle.
Other considerations	
Associated risks	The main disadvantage of fuel taxes is that the mechanism is not flexible or precise enough to reflect the way in which the vehicle is being used. In addition, when the tax is collected on a national level, coordination is needed to guarantee the allocation of the revenue at a local level. Although fuel taxes have a wide revenue potential, this is in a way diminished by the existence of fuel subsidies, which result from political pressure to keep prices low.
Main sources	CODATU 2009; Ardila-Gomez and Ortegon-Sanchez 2013; Binsted et al. 2010; Farvacque-Vitkovic and Kopanyi 2014

a. In the United States, gas taxes, the traditional mainstay of transportation funding, have not kept up with inflation. For example, states' gas taxes lost 43 percent of their value during the 1970s, 1980s, and 1990s. To complicate matters, Americans have begun to drive less in the past year, further reducing gas tax revenue (Baxandall, Wohlschlegel, and Dutzik 2009)

Table 7.5 Framework Analysis Results for Vehicle Taxation

General characteristics

Financing instrument	Vehicle taxation
Benefit	Vehicle ownership (vehicle units/type)
Beneficiary/funder	Users/private-vehicle drivers
Level of government	Local and national
Type of expense	Capital, maintenance, and operation
Periodicity	Recurrent

Financial sustainability

Stability	**Medium**. Generally paid annually, vehicle taxations usually represent the second largest revenue source from transport-related taxes. The base rate is stable over the years, representing a recurrent, robust funding source.
Political and public acceptability	**Low**. Because users generally dislike having to pay for the right of *owning* a private good, the tax is associated to a "permit" to use the road more than to ownership itself. This association, however, makes users expect that their tax money is invested in the road network; when this is not obvious, public acceptability decreases.
Convenience and administrative ease	**Medium**. Difficulties in managing this tax are associated with the need to coordinate among different levels of government in charge of revenue collection and funding allocation.

Transport sustainability

Efficiency	**Medium**. Criteria for determining vehicle taxation levels can vary depending on desired effects of the measure. Vehicle taxation could focus on engine size or be based on actual impact on road infrastructure, in which case heavy goods vehicles would be charged according to their weight.
Equity	**High**. Vehicle taxes have a redistributive effect because they are paid by vehicle owners, who generally, in developing cities, have higher incomes than public transport users. If allowed by the legislation framework, the nationally collected tax should be allocated to a local level so that the revenue can be invested in road maintenance and sustainable transport provision.
Environmental impact	**High**. To encourage a shift to more efficient vehicles, taxes can be set as a function of engine size or average carbon emissions, subjecting environmental unfriendly vehicles (including motorcycles) to a larger tax burden than eco-friendly ones. This type of vehicle taxation would not only incentivize users to buy low emission vehicles but also encourage the industry to produce vehicles with better environmental performance.

Other considerations

Associated risks	The possibility of earmarking the resources to a specific transport component depends mainly on the financial legislation rules. If not earmarked, vehicle taxation revenues will go to the national treasury, and it is difficult to guarantee that the same amount of revenue would be allocated to the local level and specifically to the transport sector (Ardila-Gomez and Ortegon-Sanchez, 2013).
Main sources	CODATU 2009; Farvacque-Vitkovic and Kopanyi 2014; Binsted et al. 2010

Table 7.6 Framework Analysis Results for Fare Box Revenue

General characteristics	
Financing instrument	Fare box revenue
Benefit	Accessibility and mobility (amount of trips)
Beneficiary/funder	Users/public transport passengers
Level of government	Local
Type of expense	Operation and maintenance
Periodicity	Recurrent
Financial sustainability	
Stability	**Medium**. Depending on patronage levels and overall mode share in the city, fare box revenue can be steady and a continuous source of revenue. This revenue is typically reinvested in the local transport system, either to cover operational costs or to support capital borrowing.
Political and public acceptability	**Medium**. In general, for good-quality systems and acceptable levels of service, fares are perceived as fair. However, fare increases—sometimes a high priority for service providers—can sometimes not be well received by the public and generate political as well as public tension.
Convenience and administrative ease	**Low**. The administration, collection, and allocation of public transit fares requires a level of technology appropriate to the revenue system and defined regulatory and institutional arrangements. The use of electronic tickets to pay into a centralized revenue system that is administrated by an independent entity has proven to be efficient and reliable. Such a system, however, requires investments in a technology platform and high institutional capacity. In addition, even with the right revenue system technology, adequately defining fares and remuneration criteria, by the public sector, can be a complex task due to political pressure and information unbalance.
Transport sustainability	
Efficiency	**Medium**. Transit fares directly charge users for the services they receive. However, because fares are defined based on technical considerations to cover operation costs, operational inefficiencies by the service provider will result in higher fares.
Equity	**Medium**. To avoid social exclusion or undesired reductions in the use of the transport mode, fare levels must take into account price elasticity and affordability, especially for the lower-income groups. Setting fares, therefore, is a compromise between covering operating cost and making the service accessible to the entire population.
Environmental impact	**Medium**. Fare levels can have an impact on the amount of motorized travel that a person chooses to undertake. For example, travel cards that allow unlimited integrated trips might encourage travelling and CO_2 emissions. Nonetheless, integrated fares can reduce the overall cost and increase trip convenience, making public modes more attractive and perhaps reducing private car trips.

table continues next page

Table 7.6 Framework Analysis Results for Fare Box Revenue *(continued)*

Other considerations	
Associated risks	While some private or public transport system operators have managed to keep their income and expenditures balanced, others face financial gaps that can only be closed with additional funding from the public sector. The exact situation may vary among countries and between developing and industrialized countries; and comparing scenarios is difficult because of the differences in operating costs and the levels of service provided. However, in general, if fares are kept low—to allow low-income populations to access the service—fares may not cover the real operation costs, in which case public funding is necessary. Public funding might be given in the form of (i) compensation for the use of special fares for certain user categories; (ii) compensation of losses at the end of the year; or (iii) payment of an amount per trip based on operating cost. See Table 6.1 also.
Main sources	CODATU 2009; Sakamoto and Belka 2010; DeGood 2011; Binsted et al. 2010

CHAPTER 8

Indirect Benefit Instruments

Indirect benefit instruments charge actors for indirect benefits stemming from the transport investment. Section "Advertising and Employer Contributions" describes advertising (table 8.1) and employer contributions (table 8.2). A range of value capture strategies is discussed in section "Value Capture Strategies", covering land asset management and various types of developer exactions.

Advertising and Employer Contributions

Tables 8.1 and 8.2 describe advertising and employer contributions, respectively.

Table 8.1 Framework Analysis Results for Advertising

General characteristics	
Financing instrument	Advertising
Benefit	Sales increases due to more exposure
Beneficiary/funder	Advertising companies
Type of expense	Maintenance and operation
Level of government	Local
Periodicity	Recurrent
Financial sustainability	
Stability	**High.** Income from advertising on infrastructure or vehicles owned by the government represents a stable financing mechanism that can be used to increase funding for operation and maintenance, in particular for cities with publicity space in areas that are of very high value to the publicity sector.
Political and public acceptability	**High.** Although there might be some opposition due to visual contamination and deterioration of the institutional image of the system, in general this instrument is not perceived badly by the public or the administration in office.

table continues next page

Table 8.1 Framework Analysis Results for Advertising *(continued)*

Convenience and administrative ease	**Medium**. Implementation requires coordination among agents and negotiations with the private sector going to advertise.
Transport sustainability	
Efficiency	**Low**. Although the instrument takes advantage of the benefit for the advertising company that ads are exposed to a large number of people, the instrument's efficiency is not directly related with transport benefits or costs.
Equity	**Low**. The instrument allows taking funding from the private sector to invest in public transport and public space infrastructure maintenance and cleaning.
Environmental impact	**Medium**. Although advertising itself does not have any direct effect on nonmotorized mode use or emission reductions, initiatives for bicycle schemes have been financed partly due to public–private partnerships (PPPs) between transport authorities and advertising agencies.
Other considerations	
Associated risks	–
Main sources	CODATU 2009; Sakamoto and Belka 2010

Table 8.2 Framework Analysis Results for Employer Contributions

General characteristics	
Financing instrument	Employer contributions
Benefit	Increases in access for employees
Beneficiary/funder	Employers
Level of government	Local
Type of expense	Maintenance and operation
Periodicity	Recurrent
Financial sustainability	
Stability	**High**. Contributing employers and personnel size are relatively stable over time.
Political and public acceptability	**Medium**. Although it might be difficult at first to get employers involved, the benefits have facilitated the acceptability of this instrument.
Convenience and administrative ease	**Medium**. Although the mechanism requires the involvement of an additional agent in the definition and coordination of transport sector policies and programs, with effective coordination the instrument might have a high impact at a relative low cost to the public sector.
Transport sustainability	
Efficiency	**Medium**. The mechanism directly charges employers for the benefit of facilitating employee access to work using the public transport system. In some cases, the charge is levied on employee salaries at a rate that depends on the size of the company. Employers must give their employees transport subsidies or free travel on public transport.

table continues next page

Table 8.2 Framework Analysis Results for Employer Contributions *(continued)*

	Employer contributions can be presented as voluntary service provision, which has an indirect effect on overall transport finances by encouraging the use of nonmotorized and public transport modes. Other associated examples such as Transport Demand Management (TDM) policies (that is, a parking cash-out program) compensate employers willing to give up their free parking space. The money can be used for carpooling or public transport.
Equity	**Medium.** Employer contributions are taxes paid by businesses either directly to the local government or to their employees as a transport fare subsidy. Companies must define mobility plans that encourage carpooling, car-sharing, and the use of nonmotorized modes, public transport, and the combination of different available modes.
Environmental impact	**Medium.** The instrument impacts mode selection by promoting the use of more environmentally efficient modes (fewer emissions per passenger) or nonmotorized modes.
Other considerations	
Associated risks	–
Main sources	CODATU 2009; Sakamoto and Belka 2010; Binsted et al. 2010

Value Capture Strategies

Value capture strategies[1] comprise several mechanisms that have the same basic financing rationale, but important differences in design and implementation. The key principle behind value capture strategies is that those who benefit from transport improvements (even if they are not users) should pay for the respective investments.

Several studies have focused on quantifying these benefits from transport improvements, for example, in terms of the increases in property values, which have been estimated at around 5–10 percent for residential and between 10 and 30 percent for commercial uses (CODATU 2009).[2] With appropriate design and management, land-based value capture financing is a good alternative for widening the tax base and ensuring continuous revenue for local or central governments. Moreover, because land-based financing relates to sustainability and the need to integrate transport and land planning policies, the instrument presents great potential for urban infrastructure financing, especially in developing countries where cities are growing rapidly. Value capture instruments, however, are slightly controversial because currently no standardized way exists to assess the different benefits created by transport system developments. Moreover, successful implementation of these instruments requires decentralization and well-functioning governance structures (Medda 2011).

As shown in table 8.3, land-based value capture financing mechanisms can be classified in three categories, with two kinds of beneficiaries: (i) added value capture mechanism and (ii) land asset management, both with land or property

Table 8.3 Overview of Value Capture Financing Mechanisms

Added Value Capture Mechanisms	*Land Asset Management*	*Developer Exactions*
Beneficiary: land or property owners	*Beneficiary: land or property owners*	*Beneficiary: developers*
Land value taxes/betterment levies. Capture value growth (price increases) resulting from the increases in accessibility and reductions in transport costs due to the development of transport infrastructure. **Tax increment financing**. Capture the estimated increase in property tax revenue resulting from the residential and commercial developments induced by the project **Special assessment**. Capture the special benefits, received within a district, that exceed the overall general benefit. **Transportation utility fees**. Capture the added value in terms of the increase in transport "use" based on a certain characteristic of the property.	**Acquisition and sale of land under specific conditions**. Involves the acquisition of land at market value (at a "without project" price), before the general public is informed of the decision to develop a project. Next, the land is sold to private developers at a "with-project" market price, which captures the added value of the benefits. **Land readjustment schemes**. Landowners pool their land to assemble a larger plot or the government acquires the land. A portion of the plot is sold to raise funds to finance partially public infrastructure development costs.	**Development impact fees**. Paid by developers for the costs of extending public infrastructure for new developments. **Negotiated exactions**. Paid by developers in return for receiving access benefits to the infrastructure project that is being developed; contributions by developers include land or the installation of public infrastructure. **Joint development**. Public–private partnership (PPP) or other formal arrangement to decrease the costs of constructing or operating public transportation. **Air rights**. Developers receive on-site development opportunities, on top of existing or new projects, in exchange for a financial contribution or future additional property and income taxes.

Source: Suzuki et al 2015, Zhao and Levinson 2012, and (Zhao, Das, and Larson 2012

owners as the beneficiaries; and (iii) developer exactions, with developers as the beneficiaries.

While the land-based financing instruments present a range of opportunities, inequality is an issue because the very areas where charging land value taxes would be feasible are usually not the areas most in need of transport project development. Similarly, developer contributions by nature indicate that their payments are confined to growth areas.

Figure 8.1 presents an overview of the value capture strategies and shows their spatial distribution. The image illustrates how transportation improvements may create value in different ways, suggesting that multiple value capture policies can be used simultaneously to capture that value. However, to achieve sustainability and to keep the economic rationale of development, it is important to guarantee that the total value captured does not exceed the total benefits created by the project (Lari et al. 2009).

Added Value Capture Mechanisms

Tables 8.4 through 8.7 present the four mechanisms to capture the added value resulting from a transport investment: land value taxes (or betterment levies, table 8.4), tax increment financing (TIF, table 8.5), special assessment (SA, table 8.6), and transportation utility fees (TUF, table 8.7).

Figure 8.1 Value Capture Strategies and Spatial Distribution

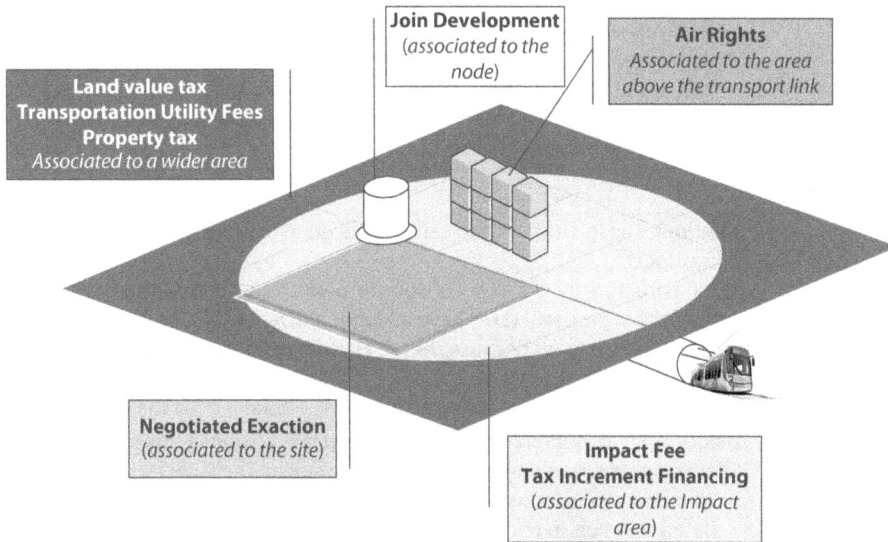

Source: Authors adaptation from Lari et al. 2009.

Table 8.4 Framework Analysis Results for Land Value Taxation and Betterment Levies

General characteristics	
Financing instrument	Land value taxation/betterment levy
Benefit	Land value growth (price increase)
Beneficiary/funder	Land/property owners
Level of government	Local
Type of expense	Capital and maintenance
Periodicity	Up front
Financial sustainability	
Stability	**Medium.** When the levy is used to charge a large area or even the whole city, its broad base implies a relatively low tax rate is possible. The instrument is also relatively stable because property values in general are not very sensitive to economic cycles[a] and the tax is difficult to avoid in the sense that the properties are immovable and cannot be relocated to a nontaxable area (Bird and Slack 2004; Sakamoto and Belka 2010). The instrument has moderate growth potential and represents a long-term continuous revenue source.

table continues next page

Table 8.4 Framework Analysis Results for Land Value Taxation and Betterment Levies (continued)

Political and public acceptability	**Low**. Acceptability is recognized as this instrument's major difficulty. The instrument's wide base implies that a very large segment of the local population is affected by the tax. The tax may be perceived as an additional tax on property.
Convenience and administrative ease	**Low**. The main difficulties are related to estimating the added value that the transport project brings to each land parcel. Estimating procedures to establish these values are usually administratively costly and legally complicated. From an institutional capacity perspective, land value taxes are relatively easy to implement, especially if well-established tax administration systems are in place and robust markets exists. However, implementation does require a complete and up to date property and land database. To guarantee compliance, it is recommended to maintain an independent and neutral source of property assessment.

Transport sustainability

Efficiency	**Medium**. The instrument can capture the general benefit from the new transport infrastructure in all zones. For specific projects, it can be argued that residential property taxes have a higher efficiency than nonresidential (commercial) taxes because they are paid by people (owners and customers) that generally live elsewhere and are just partially obtaining a benefit from the investment.
Equity	**Medium**. For geographic equity, land-based taxes generally favor central city areas, where development intensities are higher. The taxes also charge more commercial and industrial property than residential property. If defined based on value, in terms of property type, the tax will have a distributive effect by charging more to properties with higher values. In that case the equity effect is favorable as the tax is progressive.
Environmental impact	**Medium**. The instrument's impact on the environment is highly dependent on the type of infrastructure developed. If the project is associated with public transport, it will have a positive environmental impact. Road maintenance also has a positive effect in improving operating conditions. Increases in road capacity, however, generally increase demand due to induced and attracted demand, in which case the environmental impact would not be overall positive.

Other considerations

Associated risks	Although regarded as difficult due to political acceptability, there have been successful examples of different approaches for charging betterment levies. One example is in Bogota, where street and bridge improvements were packaged into a citywide bundle of public works projects financed partly via a citywide betterment fee that did not vary parcel by parcel, but was broadly differentiated by benefit zone. Despite its political difficulties, including the complications related with the administrative component of managing the collection and use of large sums of money, it is estimated that the measure has collected billions for the city of Bogota.
Main sources	Sakamoto and Belka 2010; Peterson 2009; Smolka 2013; Medda 2011

a. However, recent experience with an asset bubble in housing suggests that major corrections in housing prices, though rare, might limit the ability of a land tax to act as a countercyclical revenue instrument.

Table 8.5 Framework Analysis Results for Tax Increment Financing

General characteristics

Financing instrument	Tax Increment Financing (TIF)
Benefit	Property tax revenue growth (within TIF district)
Beneficiary/funder	Land/property owners
Level of government	Local
Type of expense	Maintenance and operation
Periodicity	Up front

Financial sustainability

Stability	**High**. The government lends the landowner a value based on estimated future increases in tax revenue equivalent to the estimated value gain that the project will create. This allows projects to be more self-financing as it reduces the dependence on other (more costly) sources of funding, such as transfers, capital budget, or a tax increase.
	The loan can be for up to ten years, and the interest rates are low. There are three methods to fund TIF districts: bonds, pay-as-you-go methods, and intrafund loans (Lari et al. 2009). Commonly, local governments issue bonds, backed by a percentage of projected future (higher) tax collections, to capture expected future increases in tax revenue within a certain area.
Political and public acceptability	**Medium**. The instrument has a narrow tax base and therefore low political visibility. TIF districts are also accepted by developers as they may allow development projects to move forward.
Convenience and administrative ease	**Low**. The administrative feasibility of TIF district implementation is low. Implementation requires several steps, including needs assessment, formulation of a (re)development plan, plan adoption, and project monitoring, each of which can be time consuming. In addition, TIF arrangements require constant monitoring by local finance departments.

Transport sustainability

Efficiency	**Medium**. TIFs are used to promote densification in the vicinity of transport infrastructure and capture the benefit of development expansion reflected in the increase in property/land tax generated from that land. The new construction generates a tax increment and an increase in transport usage. Private investors are encouraged to invest in TIF-designated zones because they are assured that their taxes will finance the development of the area, thus providing a net financial gain. However, this condition might depend on the level of productivity of the area.
Equity	**Low**. The development of a very specific location might come at the expense of development in the rest of the area. Defining the area of influence is difficult and may result in overlapping areas that would result in overcharging some zones.
Environmental impact	**Medium**. Land value taxes also provide an incentive for landowners to develop the properties to improve their use, thus increasing the city's density.

table continues next page

Sustainable Urban Transport Financing from the Sidewalk to the Subway
http://dx.doi.org/10.1596/978-1-4648-0756-5

Table 8.5 Framework Analysis Results for Tax Increment Financing *(continued)*

Other considerations	
Associated risks	Perceived abuse of the mechanism in a given jurisdictions will result in a sceptic view of the mechanism, as it will appear as a "corporate hand-out" or a way to channel subsidy funds to politically favored private firms. Also, the tool requires robust real estate and economic conditions and considerations regarding complementing mechanisms (Santos 2013) for potential future operations and maintenance funding.
Main sources	Zhao and Levinson 2012; DeGood 2011; Santos 2013; Lari et al. 2009

Note: This concept is common in Australia (where it is known as "Value Increment Financing" or VIF) and in the United States (known as "Tax Increment Financing" or TIF).

Table 8.6 Framework Analysis Results for Special Assessment

General characteristics	
Financing instrument	Special Assessment (SA)
Benefit	Assessed special benefits
Beneficiary/funder	Land/property owners
Level of government	Local
Type of expense	Maintenance and operation
Periodicity	Up front
Financial sustainability	
Stability	**Medium**. The instrument aims to charge for "excessive" benefits in a specific, special area; it has a narrow base and will require a relative high rate. However, if property owners within the district agree with the identified benefits and are willing to pay the high rates, the tool can expand substantially the available local capital budget for initial investments on public infrastructure such as streets, traffic lights, street lights, sewer and water systems, parks, and other community facilities. The tool is considered a relatively revenue-certain form of financing, since property owners typically pay their assessments with their property taxes. The tool is also flexible so it can be adapted to changes in projects' costs or macroeconomic situations such as inflation; however, the financing will only last for the duration of the assessment period.
Political and public acceptability	**Medium**. Because of its narrow base, only a relatively small group of people are involved. However, different agents might need extra evidence to be convinced of the value or necessity of adopting special assessments as an instrument of transportation finance before the charges become politically feasible. Also, in recent years, property owners have been challenging the methodology for assessing the benefits and rates.
Convenience and administrative ease	**Low**. The main difficulty with the implementation of this instrument is defining which properties receive a "disproportionate" benefit from a certain transportation improvement and how the size of this benefit varies by location. In practice, several methods are used such as: increased value,

table continues next page

Table 8.6 Framework Analysis Results for Special Assessment *(continued)*

	distance, zone, and frontage. Once in place, administration costs will decrease as the instrument can be implemented along with current property tax assessment and collection processes
Transport sustainability	
Efficiency	**Medium**. Special assessments in general do not provide a direct signal on transport use. They do, however, provide a signal to landowners about the costs of a transportation improvement. To a certain extent, it guarantees that the additional value created by the improvement is not completely captured by the private landowners.
Equity	**Low**. The aim of the instrument is to balance geographic inequities created by general revenue forms of financing.[a] But, as they are tied to some level of benefit received and do not take into consideration ability to pay, the charge can be slightly regressive, in terms of placing a greater effective tax burden on lower-income households. The instrument also has different impacts on commercial versus residential properties, creating greater, more tangible, benefits for the first.
Environmental impact	**Low**. No direct impact on mode selection or travel patterns.
Other considerations	
Associated risks	Special assessment districts for road improvements are found in parts of some rural states, where fiscal capacity is more limited. Property owners are then assessed for the cost of the improvements. In urban areas, special assessments are used not only for some types of road maintenance and improvement but also for improvements to public transit networks.
Main sources	Zhao and Levinson 2012; DeGood 2011; Santos 2013; Lari et al. 2009

a. In some cases, entire classes of properties (such as residential) are exempted from charges under special assessment districts, as was the case with an assessment district identified for Los Angeles' Red Line subway (Stopher 1993). While this might be an expedient way of mitigating potential opposition, it does allow some potential beneficiaries to free ride on the contributions of other nonexempt property owners (Lari et al. 2009).

Table 8.7 Framework Analysis Results for Transport Utility Fees

General characteristics	
Financing instrument	Transportation Utility Fees (TUF)
Benefit	Transportation use (utility)
Beneficiary/funder	Land/property owners
Level of government	Local
Type of expense	Maintenance
Periodicity	Recurrent
Financial sustainability	
Stability	**Medium**. Relatively stable, TUFs depend on travel patterns, which although more dynamic than other criteria such as property value are relatively stable in time, at least for residential properties, guaranteeing a recurrent revenue source for the system.

table continues next page

Sustainable Urban Transport Financing from the Sidewalk to the Subway
http://dx.doi.org/10.1596/978-1-4648-0756-5

Table 8.7 Framework Analysis Results for Transport Utility Feess *(continued)*

Political and public acceptability	**Low.** Like other financing mechanisms, TUFs will both positively and negatively affect groups. However, if set correctly, higher fees will have to be paid by properties that attract and generate more trips, which generally corresponds to commercial properties. As commercial groups have more political power, this might reduce acceptability.
Convenience and administrative ease	**Low.** For rented properties, it is difficult to define whether to charge the owner or the occupants. Based on the benefit principle, occupants should be charged, but for administrative reasons it would be easier to charge the owners. Administration also requires technical capacity; an agency has to estimate trips and have a complete and updated land-use property classification. In addition, the fee should be charged within a relative short time period, which would increase the workload for collection. Finally, enforcement and compliance control is difficult, given that service restriction due to lack of payment is not possible.

Transport sustainability

Efficiency	**High.** Based on the concept of treating transportation as a utility, properties are charged depending on their level of use of the system. Properties that generate more trips "consume" more transportation infrastructure use; they are therefore more responsible for its deterioration and thus are expected to pay larger contributions to maintenance expenses. The basis for the utility fee is the estimated number of trip ends associated with each property.[a] Residential trip rates can be done per unit or based on land area or frontage; commercial rates can be per gross area or per employee. Because of the periodic nature of the revenue, it should be used to cover periodic expenses such as maintenance. The fee's optimum level should then be defined based on the maintenance needs for a defined time period.
Equity	**Low.** The tool can redistribute costs and correct some of the inefficiencies associated with property taxes, such as residential properties paying more than commercial properties and large trip generators (church, stadiums, and public offices) being exempt. However, it is very likely that commercial properties pass the extra costs from the fee on to their customers, for whom it might have a regressive effect. To increase fairness, some corrections such as defining maximum amounts of trips, exempting properties that do not own a car, and using higher charges for heavier vehicles can be introduced.
Environmental impact	**Medium.** TUFs create an incentive to travel less, which would have a positive impact on emission reductions.

Other considerations

Associated risks	Since the charge varies according to land use and is higher for commercial land uses that generate more trips, the charge may have an effect on land use when commercial entities move to areas without a utility fee.
Main sources	Zhao and Levinson 2012; Lari et al. 2009

a. Using the procedures found in the *Trip Generation* manual published by the Institute of Transportation Engineers (2003) (Junge and Levinson 2012).

Land Asset Management

As described in table 8.3, land asset management involves the acquisition and sale of land under specific conditions. First the land is acquired at market value (at a "without project" price), before the general public is informed of the decision to develop a project. Next, the land is sold to private developers at a "with-project" market price, which captures the added value of the benefits.

Land asset management also covers the use of **land readjustment schemes**, which are schemes developed to split between public and private sector the value created from infrastructure development. The scheme, which has been widely used in Japan, Korea, and India, consists of public authorities acquiring undeveloped land at current-use value, installing infrastructure systems, and then returning well-defined proportions of the finished land to the original developer. Alternatively, land owners pool the land and sell a portion to finance public infrastructure development. This scheme is used less often due to low trust levels between developers and government (Peterson 2009).

Developer Exactions

The four developer exactions—Development Impact Fees (DIF), Negotiated Exactions (NE), Joint Development (JD), and air rights—(tables 8.8–8.11) are all based on benefits to the developers. Among these, DIF (table 8.8) are paid by developers for the costs of extending public infrastructure for new developments. In the case of transport projects, the developers receive as benefit the opportunity to construct a project off-site of the transport project (such as local roads, schools, or parks). DIFs are generally estimated using formal calculations of the public service costs.

Table 8.8 Framework Analysis Results for Development Impact Fees

General characteristics	
Financing instrument	Development impact fees
Benefit	Off-site development opportunities
Beneficiary/funder	Developers
Level of government	Local
Type of expense	Capital
Periodicity	Up front
Financial sustainability	
Stability	**Medium**. The fee represents a one-time, up-front charge designed to recover the systemwide public infrastructure costs associated with growth. The fees are associated with new developments, which means beneficiaries are limited within an area and the base rate is narrow. The stability of the revenue is linked to the demand for new housing and/or commercial space. Hence, it can be affected by cyclical movements in real estate markets and the economy.

table continues next page

Table 8.8 Framework Analysis Results for Development Impact Fees *(continued)*

Political and public acceptability	**Medium**. Among residents, acceptance may be high as residents perceive it as a release from the responsibility of assuming the cost of providing infrastructure for the new developments. For the same reason, developers' acceptability is lower because they perceive it as an increase in their costs. Opposition from developers may be minimal when there is a strong demand for new development within the jurisdiction.
Convenience and administrative ease	**Medium**. The value of the development impact fee, to be paid by the developer, can be estimated relatively accurately. Administrative costs are fairly low, since much of the information required to calculate appropriate fee levels can be collected from a local government's planning and/or public works department. Compliance costs should also be fairly low. The process of obtaining developer contributions, however, is complex and slow. This is because it usually involves several stakeholders, which can lead to delays in the overall planning process.
Transport sustainability	
Efficiency	**Medium**. Growth generates demand for systemwide expansions of infrastructure capacity for roads, water supply, wastewater removal, parks, and other facilities. Impact fees are a tool to make developers pay the cost of extending the system wide infrastructure to the new project site. Through this mechanism, developers are committed to secure provision of, or improvements to, the infrastructure necessary to meet the mobility needs of the new development. It also sends a signal to local government officials to only expand infrastructure networks where the cost can be recovered.
Equity	**Medium**. In principle, the mechanism could have a positive effect on equity by making the private sector contribute to the infrastructure supply of "public" services; however, depending on the characteristics of the area, impact fees could create a regressive distribution of costs for financing infrastructure.
Environmental impact	**Low**. The instrument does not directly internalize any of the negative externalities associated with transport. It does not evidently give incentives toward the shift to more sustainable modes.
Other considerations	
Associated risks	An unintended effect may be that builders in desirable markets could ignore lower-income households and turn their attention to more high-income segments of the market when they cannot recover costs associated with high, fixed levels of impact fees
Main sources	Zhao and Levinson 2012; Lari et al. 2009

Negotiated Exactions (table 8.9) are generally negotiated under more flexible conditions than the DIFs. The negotiated exactions are paid by developers in return for receiving access benefits through the infrastructure project that is being developed. The developers can contribute by giving up land or installing, at their own expense, the public infrastructure needed.

Table 8.9 Framework Analysis Results for Negotiated Exactions

General characteristics	
Financing Instrument	Negotiated exactions
Benefit	On-site access benefits
Beneficiary/funder	Developers
Level of government	Local
Type of expense	Capital, maintenance, and operation
Periodicity	Up front and recurrent

Financial sustainability	
Stability	**Medium.** Exactions, negotiated during the development approval process, are an attractive means to ensure the provision of needed infrastructure in high-growth areas. At the local level, some freedom exists to adjust the level of charges to allow revenues to keep up with projected levels of inflation, income growth, and growth. Negotiated exactions tend to be subject to cyclical trends in real estate markets and hence are only as predictable as short-term trends in markets for different types of real estate.
Political and public acceptability	**Medium.** Negotiated exactions may be politically feasible as their narrow base means that few people will be subjected to them. The developers' perception is more positive, as the ability to negotiate the level of required exactions may allow more flexibility to meet the needs of both developers and local jurisdictions, while avoiding costly delays in the development process.
Convenience and administrative ease	**Medium.** Administratively, negotiated exactions are relatively simple, as they can be managed by most planning boards and local government staff in the usual process of development permitting. The compliance cost should also be low as exactions apply mostly to new development and entail few compliance requirements, except perhaps where their legality is challenged.

Transport sustainability	
Efficiency	**Medium.** Negotiated exactions achieve a proper balance between contributions and benefits received, which makes them efficient in the allocation of resources to infrastructure. On the other hand, since exactions tend to take the form of one-time, fixed charges, they are unable to send price signals to users regarding the variable costs of infrastructure use. The developer contribution mechanism is flexible and it allows the government to negotiate the most beneficial package.
Equity	**Medium.** Negotiated exactions can provide benefits to those who are asked to contribute toward infrastructure provision and in that sense ensure benefit equity. Because of the one-time nature of the charge, concerns have been raised regarding the intergenerational equity if successive generations of residents are allowed to free ride on infrastructure paid for initially by residents of new developments. However, the degree of free riding is likely to be small if exactions are used primarily to finance on-site transportation improvements or improvements in the immediate vicinity.

table continues next page

Table 8.9 Framework Analysis Results for Negotiated Exactions *(continued)*

General characteristics	
Environmental impact	**Low.** No specific relation to reducing externalities or promoting modal shift. However, as negotiated exactions promote densification, they also promote more sustainable travel patterns such as shorter trips for certain activities.
Other considerations	
Associated risks	
Main sources	Zhao and Levinson 2012; Lari et al. 2009

The third type of developer exaction, Joint Development (JD), is public–private partnership (PPP)[3] or other formal arrangement aimed at decreasing the costs of constructing or operating public transportation improvements by engaging with an adjacent (in spatial terms) private real estate development through diverse collaboration methods.[4] Because, strictly speaking, a JD can only be called a PPP when the private sector is contractually involved for the joint financing of the project, other types of JD arrangements are available. An example is the sale or lease of land or development rights by the public sector to collect revenue. In general, JDs may involve the private sector (i) paying fees to the public sector, (ii) sharing development costs, or (iii) assuming total development costs on publicly owned land.

Joint development has been mostly used for investments in public transport and roads in high-density areas because of the positive impacts (at least under certain circumstances) of the project developments on nearby land values (especially in the case of high-speed rail stations). Joint developments can be categorized based on the property ownership, whether public or private. Publicly owned properties that are being underutilized can be sold or leased, to give the governments a budget increase at a specific moment (from sales) and/or continuous income for a given period of time (lease). Privately owned land can be used as a contribution by the private sector in exchange for development rights. Table 8.10 presents an overview of joint development types and their impacts on funds and benefits.

Using joint development mechanisms presents a comparative advantage because the definition and identification of impacts do not have to be so precise, as there is a predefined cooperation arrangement between the public agency and the private sector. Moreover, leasing arrangements increase the public sector's leverage for raising land related revenue, as well as its flexibility in motivating changes in land use and the local economy, which also has important consequences for transport requirements. The benefit analysis of joint development mechanisms is presented in table 8.11.

Finally, with air rights (table 8.12), developers receive on-site development opportunities, on top of existing or new projects, in exchange for a financial contribution or future additional property and income taxes.

Table 8.10 Joint Development Categories by Ownership Features

Ownership Features		Impact on Funds	Benefits
Publicly owned property/land	Land sale	Private sector pays a one-time lump sum for land.	Provides a large amount of capital available for immediate infrastructure development.
	Land lease	Private sector pays a rent for the land over a period of time, which can be used as a steady revenue to offset operating costs or capital improvements with freedom to renegotiate rent payments based on property value changes.	Better assembly and more control over timing, pace, and character of future development surrounding transport projects.
	Development rights sale/lease	Private sector pays for the right to develop commercial, industrial, or residential facilities on land adjacent to transport facilities.	Increase public agencies' revenues and encourage development on certain areas. Unless a previous profit-sharing agreement between public and private sector exists, the private sector retains all the revenue generated from the development.
	Development rights award	Private sector pays for the total cost of developing transit infrastructure and receives the right to recover costs through real estate development.	Development of transit infrastructure.
Privately owned property	Development rights (usage changes or density bonuses)	Private sector contributes with land, funds, or cost sharing in exchange for the development rights.	

Source: Lari et al. 2009.

Table 8.11 Framework Analysis Results for Joint Development

General characteristics	
Financing instrument	Joint development
Benefit	Development privileges
Beneficiary/funder	Developers
Level of government	Local and national
Type of expense	Capital, maintenance, and operation
Periodicity	Up front and recurrent

table continues next page

Table 8.11 Framework Analysis Results for Joint Development *(continued)*

Financial sustainability

Stability	**Medium**. The predictability of revenue from this instrument depends on the structure of the payment stream; a one-time lump-sum payment (which must be defined through legally enforceable lease or purchase agreements) will be more predictable than other financing tools that depend on demand levels or that involve a series of future payments that depend on market behavior. In general, the stability of the revenue for this mechanism is determined by either demand or economic conditions. If the revenue level is linked to demand levels or traffic volumes, demand changes will reduce fare revenue. For real estate developments, the stability depends on economic conditions. However, the flexibility of joint development schemes allows the revenues to be structured to adapt to inflation and other economic issues.
Political and public acceptability	**Medium**. For decision makers, the scheme may be more attractive than a tax increase due to the apparent low public funding it requires. However, the public may perceive the arrangements as unfair because they benefit the private sector in a greater proportion than the general public. Scholars' opinion is also divided as some regard the scheme as an effective way to involve the public and private sector with a balanced distribution of cost and benefits and responsibilities and risks, while others have concerns about possible abuse of power by both the public and private sector to obtain extremely large benefits from transportation project development.
	Political feasibility also depends on local characteristics, such as flexibility for government interventions and participation in land and property markets. Moreover, political concerns may arise if the use of joint development schemes alters project development planning or the definition of priorities.
Convenience and administrative ease	**Low**. Administration requires coordination among public and private agencies and involves associated transaction costs. Success relies on significant planning and coordination to define appropriate policies before the project begins and during implementation. Administration also requires strong capacities from the public sector professionals in charge of overseeing bidding processes timelines, efficiency, and safety.

Transport sustainability

Efficiency	**High**. Joint developments link the cost of infrastructure development with the benefits received by developers or owners. Use of joint developments improves economic efficiency by providing more accurate price signals for societal marginal costs and benefits of transit improvement through internalizing its positive externalities. Use also promotes local economic development through increases in employment, business growth, and improved accessibility. It further allows the public sector to pass some risk to the private sector, to access private financing, and to take advantage of private sector efficiency, expertise, and innovative capacity and scale economies. Joint developments also increase patronage due to clustered services, which increases revenue.[a]

table continues next page

Table 8.11 Framework Analysis Results for Joint Development *(continued)*

Equity	**Medium**. Since the agreement between public and private sector is market driven, the mechanism is perceived as equitable. The private sector participates in the project with a contribution that it has quantified as proportional to the received benefit. Tax payers have argued that too many benefits can be given to the private sector. This perception is supported by a lack of transparency around the information related with the joint development. However, if many of the owners of properties located near the project have high incomes, the instrument is defined as progressive.
Environmental impact	**Medium**. Densification around a specific node promotes more sustainable travel patterns and mode use.
Other considerations	
Associated risks	The private sector will always be interested in developing projects with higher revenue potentials. However, smaller projects or projects with higher risks still have to be considered to have a fair distribution of services across zones and modes.
Main sources	Zhao and Levinson 2012; Lari et al. 2009

a. It was found that every 1,000 square feet of new commercial space near a rail station generated an additional six transit trips a day, or an additional US$11.4 million (in 1982 dollars) in annual fare income.

Table 8.12 Framework Analysis Results for Air Rights

General characteristics	
Financing instrument	Air rights
Benefit	On-site development opportunities
Beneficiary/funder	Developers
Level of government	Local and national
Type of expense	Maintenance and operation
Periodicity	Up front and recurrent
Financial sustainability	
Stability	**Medium**. The sale or lease of development rights in a project's airspace captures some of the value created by the transportation improvement and can finance some or all of its costs. Air right developments are relatively adequate and predictable; however, this development is driven by market factors and therefore is less stable and more susceptible to slumps in the real estate market. In extreme conditions, lease payments may become more difficult to collect.
Political and public acceptability	**Medium**. Developer's acceptability is high because the opportunity to develop in higher densities in desired locations (with high demand) is commercially appealing. Public acceptability is relatively high because air rights charge a limited group of properties within a jurisdiction, meaning that most taxpayers are not involved. However, air right development usually requires high densities to be feasible, which means adjacent property owners may resist the disruption in their surroundings.

table continues next page

Sustainable Urban Transport Financing from the Sidewalk to the Subway
http://dx.doi.org/10.1596/978-1-4648-0756-5

Table 8.12 Framework Analysis Results for Air Rights *(continued)*

Convenience and administrative ease	**Low**. Air right development is administratively more complex than several of the other value capture policies. The instrument requires additional marketing and legal services skills to establish air rights and negotiate them with private tenants. Most public transit providers and transportation departments may not have this type of expertise within the organization.
Transport sustainability	
Efficiency	**Medium**. The accessibility advantage of a strategic location makes the airspace above the transport facility highly valuable and attractive for new developments. Private developers wishing to excite this opportunity should pay rents or leases proportional to the benefits received. Public sector infrastructure providers receive signals about the proper location and time of the investment from contributors who reveal their willingness to pay through a market transaction. However, the main criteria leading this development are market incentives, which are not necessarily related with sustainable travel behaviors.
Equity	**Medium**. Developers are paying for the benefit, which is usable space in a high-access location. However, in terms of geographic equity, air rights provide further development to areas already in highly demand. If densification is not linked with transit but with private vehicles, it can create accessibility issues for the residents of the areas.
Environmental impact	**Medium**. Densification and diverse land uses, especially if linked with the development of transit networks, have very positive effects in terms of promoting short trips that can be undertaken using nonmotorized modes.
Other considerations	
Associated risks	–
Main sources	Zhao and Levinson 2012; Lari et al. 2009

Notes

1. The analysis of the instruments in this section is largely based on similar analysis performed by (Lari et al. 2009), (Zhao and Levinson 2012), (Zhao, Das, and Larson 2012), (CODATU 2009), (Sakamoto and Belka 2010), and (Suzuki et al. 2015).

2. Instruments, such as betterment levies, have been implemented by public authorities to capture around 30–60 percent of land value gains (Peterson 2009).

3. Public–private partnership description not accurate in all cases (Zhao, Das, and Larson 2012).

4. National Council for Urban Economic Development 1989 as cited by (Zhao, Das, and Larson 2012).

CHAPTER 9

Public–Private Partnerships

Public–Private Partnerships (PPPs) allow the public sector to obtain resources from the private sector through a contractual agreement; it is a financing mechanism that can secure funding for the overall life cycle of the project (including construction, modernization, maintenance, operation, and service provision). Because a PPP simultaneously addresses private and public sector interests, it is regarded as a very effective instrument for local authorities to finance infrastructure. The public sector's main objective is to protect taxpayer interests and increase the overall funding budget so that projects in all sectors can be developed (health, education, transport). By sharing design, construction, operating, and financing risks, the public sector benefits from the presumable advantages of the private sector such as economies of scale, efficiency-driven performance due to their obligation to reward shareholders, flexibility in regulation, and knowhow and extensive experience in complex industrial and commercial activities. From the private sector's perspective, its main motivation is the participation in projects of the magnitude of transport projects and having the guarantees provided by the public sector (Gwilliam 2000). Ideally, PPPs combine the security and commitment of the public sector with the expertise and efficiency of the private sector, while distributing risks and responsibilities between both parties according to their capabilities for managing them (World Bank 2013).

The main criticism of PPPs is that careful management is required. The public sector's main responsibility is defining clear and robust mechanisms (such as contracts and information flows) to allow it to demand good practices from the private sector. Contracts are the main mechanism to prevent service deterioration that might result from private sector intentions to reduce costs to maximize profits. They also allow renegotiations and accounts settlements should the private sector fail to deliver the project.

The different types of PPPs, varying from short-term management contracts to complex partnership, are illustrated in figure 9.1 and table 9.1.

Figure 9.1 Types of Public–Private Partnerships

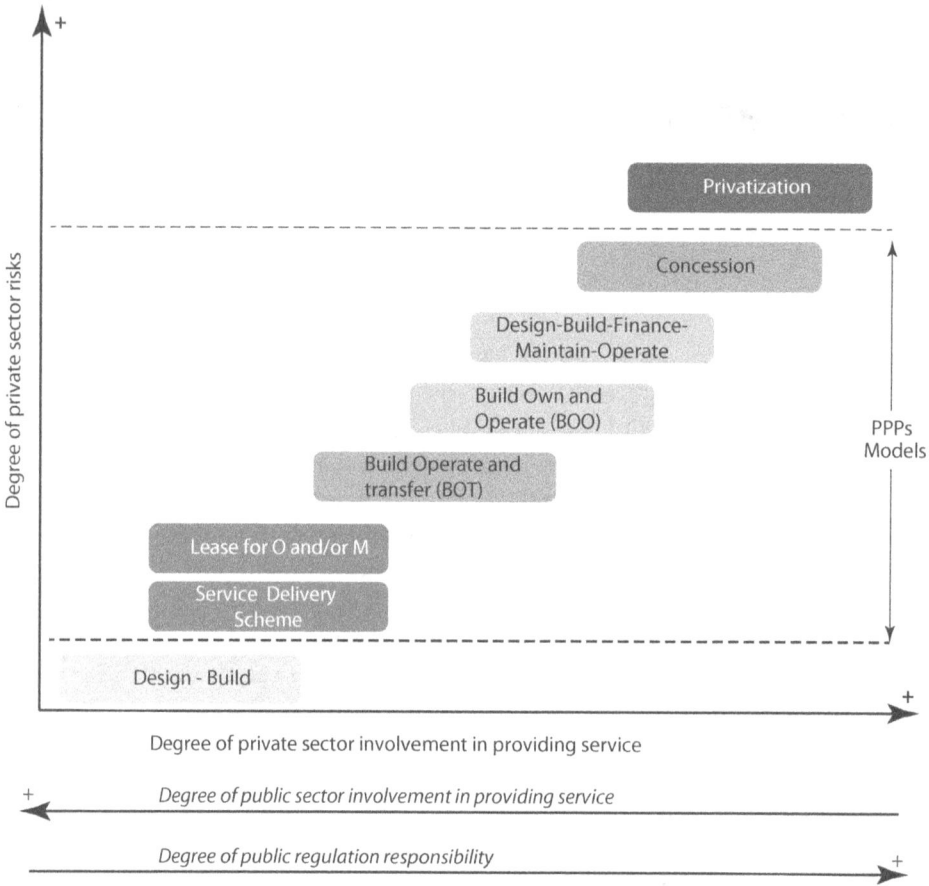

Source: Authors based on Sakamoto and Belka 2010; CODATU 2009; Zegras 2006.

Table 9.1 Types of Public–Private Partnerships

Type of partnership	Type of project	Contract details	Fees	Risk
Design and build	Infrastructure projects	Construction project tendered and private contractor selected by competitive bidding process	Fixed fee agreed in the bid for planning and construction	Contractor is responsible for the risk during planning and construction
Service delivery scheme	Bus operation	As a rule of thumb, ideally should be done by private operators in well-regulated market, tendered under competitive conditions.	Will be set based on technical criteria	The risk of demand is transferred to the private sector

table continues next page

Table 9.1 Types of Public–Private Partnerships *(continued)*

Type of partnership	Type of project	Contract details	Fees	Risk
		The contract must demand from the private firm high service standards. The public sector must invest in infrastructure with priority measures.		
Service delivery scheme	Road maintenance	Performance-based contracts upon defined standards for road features		
Lease to private sector for the operation of an existing road (or infrastructure)	Service operation or asset maintenance	Several types of contracts. Public sector maintains the responsibility for the investment and has the ownership of the infrastructure. Private contractor is responsible for all the operation and maintenance responsibilities except toll revenue collection.	Public sector can hold funds in case contract terms are unfulfilled. Hence, the private operator receives "availability payments" instead of tolls	Operational risks are transferred to the operator. Public risk decreases in relation to potential lawsuits for compensation when policies to reduce traffic are successfully implemented
Build-Operate-Transfer (BOT)	Roads	Private sector both builds and operates the infrastructure. The contractor invests in infrastructure and operates it for a period of time after which ownership is reverted back to the public sector. The public sector can stipulate basic levels of service requirements. (Different from franchises, often used to provide urban rail and buses, under which private sector can define levels of service provision.)		Risk is transferred to the private sector, but public sector retains ownership
Build-Own-Operate (BOO)	Combine construction of urban transport infrastructure and services	Developer designs and builds the complete project at almost zero cost for the public sector; it operates the facility for a set period (20–30 years), after which it is transferred to the government or partner at a previously agreed-upon price or market price.	Previously agreed-upon or market price	Build-Own-Operate

table continues next page

Table 9.1 Types of Public–Private Partnerships (continued)

Type of partnership	Type of project	Contract details	Fees	Risk
		The contracts included guarantee quantity, quality, and costs.		
		A revenue stream is a prerequisite for the contract and a regulator will be appointed to follow the contract and prevent abuse of its monopoly position by the contractor.		
Design-Built-Finance-Operate (Private Finance Initiative)	Combine construction of urban transport infrastructure and services operation and/or asset maintenance	Private sector builds, owns, and operates a facility, which it sells to its users. These contracts aim to minimize the contribution of tax-payers resources and achieve value for the money. For handing back the infrastructure to the public sector it must have a specified residual life which will guarantee that investment in maintenance will not be needed for a certain amount of time.		Transfer the risk to private operator while promoting technical, financial and commercial innovation.

Source: Authors based on Sakamoto and Belka 2010; CODATU 2009; Zegras 2006.

Strictly speaking, PPPs are not a source of funding but a way of raising funds, similar to a loan but committing the lender (CODATU 2009); this feature makes the definition of benefits and beneficiaries (from a framework perspective) slightly more complicated. A simpler approach, however, to analyzing the mechanism can be made by separating the interest and benefits for each of the agents involved in PPPs, the public and the private sectors. On the one hand, public sector interest is to provide transport infrastructures and services, which means the benefit would be general and therefore must be funded by the general public. On the other hand, the private sector benefit is getting the opportunity to participate in a large business to obtain profit, and its contribution is providing funding in the short term. This means that in the long term the general public, through fares and tolls, funds the project, but in the short term the private sector provides capital to develop the project. The financial and transport sustainability attributes of PPPs are described in table 9.2.

Table 9.2 Framework Analysis Results for Public–Private Partnerships

General characteristics	
Financing instrument	Public–Private Partnerships
Benefit	General benefit/business opportunity
Beneficiary/funder	General public/private sector
Level of government	National

Financial sustainability	
Stability	**Medium**. Private sector relies on debt and asset inflation rather than income or cash flows to finance acquisitions and pay dividends to shareholders, which raises questions concerning the sustainability. The private sector also has higher borrowing costs, which means that deals will tend to lose the public money over the long term. Moreover, to attract private investment, contracts might include "noncompete" clauses as revenue protection mechanisms. In general, compensation payments might end up considerably increasing construction costs, making the projects unaffordable.
Political and public acceptability	**Medium**. In the short term, PPPs have several political benefits, such as reducing the need for governments to increase taxes to have more transport systems revenues. PPPs also alleviate budget pressure, allowing governments to invest in other sectors. Finally, it distances governments from toll increases and improves the image of the politicians, as the opening of new infrastructure projects is always well perceived.
	High. If the PPP is for public transport, given the overall benefits for citizens.
Convenience and administrative ease	**Low**. Local legislation can be defined to promote road privatization or service concession; however, caution has to be taken to guarantee that this promotion does not represent extra benefits for the private sector (Baxandall, Wohlschlegel, and Dutzik 2009).[a] Usually, these types of projects have several forecasting problems, which means high institutional capacity is required from the public sector.
	Governments and regulatory agencies have to define appropriate award mechanism, information flow channels, and regulatory and contractual frameworks to regulate the quality of the project (including levels of service and maintenance) and the firms' behaviors under noncompetitive conditions or toward the end of the concession period. Governments have to design adequate incentives for the different stages of the project to prevent underbidding in expectation of future renegotiations and to reduce the risk of privatizing profits while socializing losses. Institutional capacity has to be reflected in the coordination of institutions because multiple agencies with jurisdiction on the same area represent a barrier for the planning of integrated transport systems.
	Governments should also establish a legal framework (property rights, contract obligations, security rights), a regulatory regime (autonomous, independent), and competitive and transparent bidding mechanisms. A proper legal framework will give all parties certainty about the feasibility of the concession approach. Moreover, government must have an independent

table continues next page

Table 9.2 Framework Analysis Results for Public–Private Partnerships *(continued)*

	regulatory body free of political and industrial pressure, but with access to accurate information, in charge of enforcing existing contracts, or modifying them when needed. Lack of such a regulatory agency has led to the "privatize now, regulate later approach," which is considered to be one of the biggest problems with current concessions.[b]

Transport sustainability

Efficiency	**Medium**. Road concessions, if not integrated with road pricing policies designed to tackle congestion, limit public welfare as they reduce government capacity to decide on transport policies, and adapt supply to the changing needs of demand. Governments have to attract the private sector through the provision of guarantees, which may have a negative impact on efficiency, given that risk allocation and distribution is done under highly uncertain conditions, especially when associated with demand levels. However, the mechanism promotes the "Who Benefits Pays" principle: higher efficiency for infrastructure delivery in terms of time and resources and higher operating efficiency due to the use of innovative technologies. PPPs have the potential for construction and operational risk transfer to the private sector. Private sector's feasibility studies might prevent investment in unprofitable projects (filtering out of "white elephants") (Zegras 2006). By subcontracting certain activities, the public sector's need for specialized staff reduces.
Equity	**Low**. In PPPs for urban roads, the private operator will set toll rates and fares so that all its costs are covered and its profits maximized. High rates might force users to find detours or shift modes to avoid excessive costs. Traffic diversion caused by toll raises will affect local roads of the alternative route and patronage reduction will affect system's financial sustainability. In the end, the costs represent loses to the public sector and society as a whole. Similarly, to increase profit, private operators will choose cost reducing strategies that might compromise safety and maintenance standards. Even if high-quality standards are specified in the contracts, rigorous overseeing of the operation is required to prevent private operators from underinvesting. Situations such as financial distress or the end of contract proximity might create even more incentives for companies to not invest.
	Short-term benefits might represent intergenerational equity losses because of budget reductions in the long run and a raising of the toll rates, especially because the private sector generally has higher borrowing rates and the need to direct some revenues to shareholder profits, which will be reflected in the toll rates. This means that users and taxpayers will have to pay relatively more than the benefit they perceive.
	High. In PPPs for public transport, the high-quality standard contracts have proven to be a successful way of delivering good-quality transport, giving users equitable access to goods and services in cities.
Environmental impact	**Low**. In PPPs for urban roads, toll road layout and decisions to expand capacity (more lanes) impact urban planning in aspects such as car use dependence, emission levels, and overall contribution to global warming.

table continues next page

Table 9.2 Framework Analysis Results for Public–Private Partnerships *(continued)*

	High. In PPPs for public transport, emissions per passenger are estimated to be much less than if those individuals were to use cars. Also, the tendency toward vehicles with cleaner technologies and mechanisms to request them from operators has allowed public transport to achieve greater environmental benefits.
Other considerations	
Associated risks	Difficulties to gather funding in the short term made road privatization popular in Latin America in the 1990s,[c] and, more recently, it has increased in popularity in the United States. However, many of those privatization deals ended up in failures.[d] Failures can be related with difficulties in several areas, including lacking simplicity and clarity in bidding processes and inadequate prequalification and screening of bidders, as well as with difficulties related to contract renegotiations, risk balance and allocation, contract extensions, long-term legal frameworks, and capacity building for the regulatory body.
	Signing contracts, building facilities, and operating with positive financial conditions, however, are only signs of success if the project also has social, environmental, and economic benefits.
	Shadow tolls, although well intentioned and with a coherent economic rationale (making future generations pay for the benefit they will receive from the project), can create wrong incentives for governments, making them overextend their capacity and needs. This is because the idea of delivering projects at "no costs" is highly attractive in political terms and to gain votes.
Main sources	Sakamoto and Belka 2010; CODATU 2009; Zegras 2006, (PricewaterhouseCoopers Pvt. Ltd., 2008, DeGood 2011, Bahl et al. 2013

a. In the United States, tolling became a key element of the congestion mitigation strategy from the department of transport.
b. Enget et al. 2003a as cited by (Zegras 2006).
c. According to World Bank records, infrastructure privatization outside of the United States reached a peak of over US$110 billion per year in 1997 and 1998 (Baxandall, Wohlschlegel, and Dutzik 2009).
d. It was found that between 1982 and 2000 55 percent of privatization contracts in transportation had been renegotiated.

Bibliography

Altshuler, A. A., Gomez-Ibanez, J. A. & Howitt, A.M, 1993. Regulation for revenue: The political economy of land use exactions. Washington: The Brookings Institution and The Lincoln Institute of Land Policy.

Ardila-Gomez, A., and A. Ortegon-Sanchez, 2013. *The Finances of Bogota's Transportation System*. Paper presented at the World Conference on Transport Research, Rio de Janeiro. July 13--18. .

Ardila-Gomez, A. 2005. "La olla a presión del transporte público en Bogotá." Revista de Ingeniería No.21, Facultad de Ingeniería, Universidad de Los Andes, Bogotá.

———. 2007. "How Bogota's Public Transportation Past Is Haunting Its Future." Transportation Research Record, *Journal of the Transportation Research Board* 2038: 9–15.

———. 2008. "The Limitation of Competition in and for the Market in Public Transportation in Developing Countries: Lessons from Latin American Cities." Transportation Research Record, *Journal of the Transportation Research Board* 2048: 8–15.

———. 2012. "Nota 31. Transporte Urbano." In *Peru en el umbral de una nueva era: Lecciones y desafíos para consolidar el crecimiento económico y un desarrollo más incluyente. Notas de Política Volumen II,* - Parte 1 de 4: Crecimiento y Competitividad. edited by S. Goldmark, C. F. Jaramillo, and C. Silva-Jauregui, 555–78. Lima, Peru.: The World Bank.

Bahl, R. 2012. "Metropolitan City Finances in India: Options for a New Fiscal Architecture." International Center for Public Policy, Issue Working Paper Series, at AYSPS, GSU paper1233. International Center for Public Policy, Andrew Young School of Policy Studies, Georgia State University.

Bahl, R., and J. F. Linn, 1992. *Urban Public Finance in Developing Countries*. Oxford: s.n. Oxford University Press.

Bahl, R. W., and R. M. Bird. 2008. "Tax Policy in Developing Countries: Looking Back and Forward." *National Tax Journal* 61 (2): 279–301. (National Tax Association).

Bahl, R. W., J. F. Linn, and D. L. Wetzel. 2013. *Financing Metropolitan Governments in Developing Countries*. Cambridge, MA.: Lincoln Institute of Land Policy.

Baxandall, P., K. Wohlschlegel, and T. Dutzik. 2009. *Private Roads, Public Costs. The Facts about Toll Road Privatization and How to Protect the Public*. U.S. PIRG Education Fund. Frontier Group.

Binsted, A., D. Bongardt, H. Dalkmann, and K. Sakamoto. 2010. *Accessing Climate Finance for Sustainable Transport*. Eschborn, Germany: GTZ.

Bird, Richard M. (2001) "Setting the Stage: Municipal Finance and Intergovernmental Finance," in M.E. Freire and R.E. Stren, eds., *The Challenge of Urban Governance* (Washington: World Bank Institute).

Bird, R. M., and E. Slack. 2004. *Fiscal Aspects of Metropolitan Governance*. Toronto: International Tax Program, Institute for International Business, Joseph L. Rotman School of Management, University of Toronto.

Breithaupt, M. 2004. *Economic Instruments. Module 1d. Sustainable Transport: A Sourcebook for Policy-makers in Developing Cities*. Eschborn.: GTZ.

Buehler, R., and J. Pucher. 2011. "Making Public Transpor Financially Sustainable." *Transport Policy* 18 (1): 126–38.

Button, K. 2010. *Transport Economics*. 3rd ed. Cheltenham, UK; Northampton, MA: Edward Elgar.

Calimente, J. 2012. "Rail Integrated Communities (RIC) in Tokyo." *The Jounal of Transport and Land Use* 5 (1): 19–32.

Casella, S. 2002. *Tax Increment Financing: A Tool for Rebuilding New York*. FAICP.

Cervero, R., and K. Kockelman. 1997. "Travel Demand and the 3Ds: Density, Diversity, and Design." *Transportation Research, Part D* 2 (3): 199–219.

CODATU. 2009. *Who Pays what for Urban Transport? Handbook of Good Practices*. Mercues, France. France Quercy.

Committee on Equity Implications of Evolving Transportation Finance Mechanisms. 2011. *Equity of Evolving Transportation Finance Mechanisms*. Washington D.C. Transportation Research Board.

DeGood, K. 2011. *Thinking Outside the Farebox. Creative Approaches to Financing Transit Projects*. Washington, DC: Transportation for America.

The Economist. 2014. *Driving to an Early Grave*. January 25 Edition.

Estupinan, N., A. Gomez-Lobo, R. Munoz-Raskin, and T. Serebrisky. 2007. "Affordability and Subsidies in Public Transport: What Do We Mean? What Can Be Done?" Policy Research Working Paper, IssueWPS4440, World Bank, Washington, DC.

Farvacque-Vitkovic, C., and K. Mihaly, eds. 2014. *Municipal Finances: A Handbook for Local Governments*. Washington, DC: World Bank.

Figueroa, O. 2013. "Four Decades of Changing Transport Policy in Santiago, Chile." *Research in Transportation Economics* 40 (1):87–95.

Gomez-Ibanez, J. A. 1999. "Pricing." In *Essays in Transportation Economics and Policy: A Handbook in Honor of John R. Meyer*, edited by J. A. Gomez-Ibanez, W. B. Tye, and C. Winston, 99–136. Washington, DC: The Brookings Institution.

Gómez-Lobo, A., and J. Briones. 2012. *Incentive Structure in Transit Concession Contracts: The Case of Santiago, Chile, and London, England*. Washington, D.C. Clean Air Institute.

Gwilliam, K. 2000. "The New Economics of Sustainable Transport in Developing Countries: Incentives and Institutions." In *Analytical Transport Economics: An International Perspective*, edited by J. B. Polak and Arnold Heertige, 368–99. Cheltenham: Edward Elgar Publishing Limited.

Gwilliam, K. M. 2002. *Cities on the Move: A World Bank Urban Transport Strategy Review*, Washington, DC: World Bank.

Haubold, H. 2014. *Commuting: Who Pays the Bill? Overview of Fiscal Regimes for Commuting in Europe and Recommendations for Establishing a Level Playing Field.* Brussels: European Cycling Federation.

Institute of Transportation Engineers. 2003. Trip generation. Informational report of the Institute of Transportation Engineers. Washington, DC: Institute of Transportation Engineers, 7th edition.

James, S. and C. Nobes. 2009. *Economics of Taxation: Principles, Policies and Practice.* 9th ed. Birmingham: Fiscal Publications.

Junge, J., and D. Levinson. 2012. "Prospects for Transportation Utility Fees." *The Journal of Transport and Land Use* 5 (1): 33–47.

Kamal-Chaoui, L., E. Leman, and R. Zhang. 2009. "Urban Trends and Policy in China." OECD Regional Development Working Papers, OECD Publishing, Paris.

Kopp, A., R. Block, and A. Iimi.. 2012. *Turning the Right Corner. Ensuring Development Through a Low-Carbon Transport Sector.* Directions in Development. Washington, DC: World Bank.

Lari, A., Lari, Adeel; Levinson, David; Zhao, Zhirong (Jerry); Iacono, Michael; Aultman, Sara; Vardhan Das, Kirti; Junge, Jason; Larson, Kerstin; Scharenbroich, Michael. 2009. *Value Capture for Transportation Finance: Report to the Minnesota Legislature.* Minnesota: Center for Transportation Studies, University of Minnesota.

Lefevre, B., D. Leipziger, and M. Raifman. 2014. "The Trillion Dollar Question: Tracking Public and Private Investment in Transport." Working Paper, World Resources Institute, Washington, DC.

Leman, E. 2014. *China's Metropolitan Regions: Recent Trends and Prospects (presentation to World Bank office in Beijing).* Beijing: Chreod Ltd.

Litman, T. 2012. "Local Funding Options for Public Transportation." Submitted for presentation at the Transportation Research Board 2013 Annual Meeting, Victoria, Canada.

———. 2014. *Evaluating Transportation Equity-Guidance for Incorporating Distributional Impacts.* Victoria, Canada: Victoria Transport Policy Institute.

Mathur, O. P. D. Thakur, and N. Rajadhyaksha. 2009. *Urban Property Tax Potential in India.* New Delhi: National Institute of Public Finance and Policy.

McKinsey Global Institute. 2011. *Construyendo ciudades competitivas: La clave para el crecimiento de América Latina.* McKinsey and Company.

Medda, F. 2011. "Land Value Finances: Resources for Public Transport." In *Innovative Land and Property Taxation,* edited by Remy Sietchiping, 42–53. Nairobi, Kenya.: UN-HABITAT.

Medda, F. R., and M. Modelewska. 2010. *Land Value Capture as a Funding Source for Urban Investment. The Warsaw Metro System.* Warsaw: Ernst & Young Better Government Programme.

Meloche, J.-P., F. Vaillancourt, and S. Yilmaz. 2004. *Decentralization or Fiscal Autonomy? What Does Really Matter? Effects on Growth and Public Sector Size in European Transition Countries.* Washington, DC: World Bank. https://openknowledge.worldbank.org/handle/10986/15619, License: CC BY 3.0 Unported.

Mikesell, J. L. 2003. *Fiscal Administration: Analysis and Applications for the Public Sector.* 6th ed. Belmont, CA: Wadsworth.

Nakhooda, S. et al. 2012. *The Evolving Global Climate Finance Architecture. Climate Finance Fundamentals 2.* http://www.climatefundsupdate.org (accessed October 20, 2015).

Nantulya, V. M., and M. R. Reich. 2002. "The Neglected Epidemic: Road Traffic Injuries in Developing Countries." *British Medical Journal (BMJ)* 324 (7346): 1139–41.

Nicholson, W., and C. Snyder. 2008. *Microeconomic Theory. Basic Principles and Extensions,* 679–80. Mason, OH: Thomson.

Peterson, G. 2009. *Unlocking Land Values to Finance Urban Infrastructure.* Washington D.C.: World Bank.

PricewaterhouseCoopers Pvt. Ltd. 2008. *Urban Transportation Financing: A Strong Case for Public-Private Partnership.* PricewaterhouseCoopers Pvt. Ltd.

Replogle, M. 2008. "Road Pricing and Congestion Charging. Experience, Opportunities, Motivation." Presentation to Environmentally Sustainable Transport Conference, Environmental Defense and the Institute for Transportation and Development Policy, Singapore.

Rye, T., and S. Ison. 2005. "Overcoming Barriers to the Implementation of Car Parking Charges at UK Workplaces." *Transport Policy* 12 (1): 57–64.

Sakamoto, K., and S. Belka. 2010. *Financing Sustainable Urban Transport. Module 1f.* GTZ. Eschborn: GTZ.

Sakamoto, K., H. Dalkmann, D. Bongardt, and A. Binsted. 2010. *Accessing Climate Finance for Sustainable Transport: A practical Overview.* Eschborn, Germany: GTZ.

Santos, V. 2013. *Local Financing Tools to Promote Economic Development. Examples from across the U.S.* Presented at Hacia Desarrollo Urbano Sostenible e Inclusivo. Quito, Ecuador, Marzo 11 y 12, World Bank.

Santos, G., H. Behrendt, and A. Teytelboym. 2010. "Part II: Policy Instruments for Sustainable Road Transport." *Research in Transportation Economics* 28 (1): 46–91.

Sastre-González, J. 2012. *FINANCIACIÓN Y CALIDAD EN EL TRANSPORTE PUBLICO.* Léon, México: Congreso Las Mejores Práticas SIBRT En América Latina.

SDG. 2010. *An Introduction to Tax Increment Financing (TIF).* http://www.steerdavies-gleave.com/news-and-insights/introduction-tax-increment-financing-tif (accessed June 27, 2014).

Smolka, M. 2013. *Implementing Value Capture in Latin America. Policy and Tools for Urban Development.* Cambridge, MA: Lincoln Institute of Land Policy.

Stopher, P. R. 1993. "Financing Urban Rail Projects: The Case of Los Angeles." *Transportation* 20 (3): 229–250.

Stubbs, M. 2002. "Car Parking and Residential Development: Sustainability, Design and Planning Policy, and Public Perceptions of Parking Provision." *Journal of Urban Design* 7 (2): 213–37.

Suzuki, H., J. Murakami, Y. Hong, and B. Tamayose. 2015. *Financing Transit-Oriented Development with Land Values: Adapting Land Value Capture in Developing Countries.* Washington, DC: Urban Development Series, World Bank Group.

Tiebout, C. M. 1956. "A Pure Theory of Local Expenditures." *The Journal of Political Economy* 64 (5): 416–24.

TransitCenter and Frontier Group. 2014. *Subsidizing Congestion: The Multibillion-dollar Tax Subisidy That's Making Your Commute Worse.* New York, NY; Santa Barbara, CA: Frontier Group.

Vickerman, R. 2004. "Public and Private Initiatives in Infrastructure Provision." In: *Barriers to Sustainable Transport: Institutions, Regulation and Sustainability,* edited by P. Rietveld and R. Stough, 18–36. London.: Spon Press.

Weston, M. 2013. *Transport for London - A truly Integrated Transport Authority Delivering a World Class Bus Service.* Bogota: Mobility Fair, TfL.

———. 2013. *Planning, Connecting and Financing Cities-Now: Priorities for City Leaders.* Washington, DC: World Bank.

Wright, L. 2007. *BRT Planning Guide.* New York: Institute for Transportation and Development Policy.

Zegras, C. 2006. *Private Sector Participation in Urban Transport Infrastructure Provision. In Sustainable Transport: A Sourcebook for Developing Cities.* Module 1c. GTZ.

Zhao, Z., K. V. Das, and K. Larson. 2012. "Joint Development as a Value Capture Strategy for Public Transit Finance." *The Journal of Transport and Land Use* 5 (1): 5–17.

Zhao, Z. J., and D. Levinson. 2012." Introduction to the Special Issue on Value Capture for Transportation Finance." *The Journal of Transport and Land Use* 5 (1): 1–3.

ECO-AUDIT

Environmental Benefits Statement

The World Bank Group is committed to reducing its environmental footprint. In support of this commitment, the Publishing and Knowledge Division leverages electronic publishing options and print-on-demand technology, which is located in regional hubs worldwide. Together, these initiatives enable print runs to be lowered and shipping distances decreased, resulting in reduced paper consumption, chemical use, greenhouse gas emissions, and waste.

The Publishing and Knowledge Division follows the recommended standards for paper use set by the Green Press Initiative. The majority of our books are printed on Forest Stewardship Council (FSC)–certified paper, with nearly all containing 50–100 percent recycled content. The recycled fiber in our book paper is either unbleached or bleached using totally chlorine free (TCF), processed chlorine free (PCF), or enhanced elemental chlorine free (EECF) processes.

More information about the Bank's environmental philosophy can be found at http://crinfo.worldbank.org/wbcrinfo/node/4.

green
press
INITIATIVE

9 781464 807565